If thou would'st right the world,
And banish all its evils and its woes,
Make its wild places bloom,
And its drear deserts blossom as the rose,—
Then right thyself.
If thou would'st turn the world
From its long, lone captivity in sin,
Restore all broken hearts,
Slay grief, and let sweet consolation in,—
Turn thou thyself.
If thou would'st cure the world
Of its long sickness, end its grief and pain;
Bring in all-healing joy,
And give to the afflicted rest again,—
Then cure thyself.
If thou would'st wake the world
Out of its dream of death and dark'ning strife,
Bring it to Love and Peace,
And Light and brightness of immortal Life,—
Wake thou thyself.

—James Allen
The Path of Prosperity

RANDY J. GIBBS

YOU GET TO SAY

MAKING SENSE OF TRIALS, SETBACKS, AND NEGATIVE SURPRISES

CFI
Springville, Utah

ISBN 13: 978-1-59955-461-7

Published by CFI, an imprint of Cedar Fort, Inc., 2373 W. 700 S., Springville, UT 84663
Distributed by Cedar Fort, Inc., www.cedarfort.com

LIBRARY OF CONGRESS CATALOGING-IN-PUBLICATION DATA

Gibbs, Randy J.
  You get to say / Randy Gibbs.
    p. cm.
  Summary: Tools for coping with disappointment, trials, and setbacks.
  ISBN 978-1-59955-461-7
  1. Self-help techniques. I. Title.

  BF632.G47 2010
  248.8'6--dc22

                                  2010023935

Cover design by Danie Romrell
Cover design © 2010 by Lyle Mortimer
Edited and typeset by Heidi Doxey

Printed in the United States of America
10 9 8 7 6 5 4 3 2 1
Printed on acid-free paper

For Jack, Parker, Marley, and Sam

CONTENTS

INTRODUCTION

My wife and I were out recently with four other couples, all long-time friends. Soon the topic turned to our various trying circumstances. One had a mother struggling with lingering cancer. Another faced the prospect of turning her teenage son into the police for possession of illegal drugs. Another was recovering from painful surgery with more surgeries to follow. One couple had recently learned that their older son and his wife of only two years had decided to divorce. After comparing crosses for some time, one friend lamented, "Life sure doesn't turn out the way you expect it to, does it?" To which another responded, "Well, that all depends on what you were expecting."

And there's the rub. While we are told that God deliberately structured mortality to be a testing and trying experience, life rarely unfolds the way we expect. It is fraught with constant uncertainty, various trials, setbacks, and negative surprises we could never have predicted. It's easy to feel anxious about life, always wondering what stern challenge will come our way. To be sure, life's inevitable ups and downs raise a host of sobering questions for which there seem to be few good answers. We are even told not to ask the "why" questions because such questions have no solid answers. But this leaves us bewildered by our mortal experiences and often little productive learning occurs.

We are generally told there are few answers to our deepest questions, which only raises further confusion and more questions. "I guess what I'm passing through is supposed to be for my good," we say. "This must be a learning experience," we conclude. "But what am I supposed to learn?" The one-liner "Life is hard and then you die" sums up most of the consolatory words we receive. This philosophy is supposed to make us feel better. But it doesn't. Most of the "answers" we hear are little more than wild guesses about why God is doing this to us. The bottom line? For many people, even good people, the vicissitudes of life generate a host of puzzling and sometimes troubling questions.

God didn't intend for us to stumble about in the darkness, stunned and confused by our trials. After all, what would this really accomplish? Often, these difficult experiences only become trials because of how we interpret them, how we explain them, or what we make them mean. With clear perception and spiritual vision, our trials can become significant stepping stones toward increased learning and growth. Brigham Young said:

> You who have not passed through the trials and persecutions and drivings with this people from the beginning, but have only read about them or heard some of them related, may think "How awful it must have been and terrible to endure." You may also wonder how the Saints survived such trials at all and the thought of it all makes your heart sick, and you are ready to exclaim "I could not have endured it." I have been in the heart of it and never felt better in all my life. I never felt the presence and power of Almighty God more completely poured out upon me than in the keenest part of our trials. They appeared nothing to me.[1]

This doesn't sound like a man barely holding up beneath the weight of his trials—and he had plenty. Certainly he possessed a buoyancy and a degree of insight worthy of emulation. As this book will demonstrate, circumstances have no power to bring us down or cause unnecessary suffering, as Brigham Young would happily attest.

President Young underscores the principle that *how* we think about and respond to our challenges sets the stage for so much that follows. If learning, growth, and increased understanding are the primary purposes for our trials, shoulder-shrugging acceptance of our difficulties is not helpful. In the majority of cases, there are far more effective and productive ways to think about and react to our trials and setbacks than we realize.

As I listened to my dinner group of faithful individuals discuss their respective challenges, I heard several reasonable questions that we all wrestle with at various times in our lives:

+ How do I know when God is sending me a trial as opposed to me inadvertently bringing on my own troubles?

+ Is every setback supposed to teach me something? If so, what am I supposed to learn from a tragedy in my past?

+ Do I deserve my present trials because of my past transgressions or poor choices?

+ If my trials are supposed to be for my good, why do I feel so bad? Am I missing something?

+ I want to learn and grow from my difficulties, but how can I if I'm totally confused and shocked by what has happened?

+ How can I avoid unnecessary emotional suffering? How can I prevent a trial from mushrooming into a devastating experience?

The questions we struggle with during a stern trial are normal, natural, and appropriate. They reflect an honest desire to learn from our experience—not just survive. The old saying "What doesn't kill you will make you stronger" is often untrue. God is not trying to weed us out by testing us to our breaking point. He wants us to learn from our experiences, which happens far less than it should. Striving earnestly to learn from our experiences through humble inquiry can set the stage for powerful breakthroughs as we face and productively endure life's stern challenges.

Though we rarely realize it, we have far more influence over the impact of our mortal experiences than we think.

THE BIG FOUR

Before we can discuss productive ways of thinking and reacting to trials and setbacks, we need to clarify four different causes for our trials. Most people oversimplify the cause and purpose for their earthly misfortunes. We too easily conclude that God is somehow behind all the challenges we face, which is not only incorrect but unproductive. This introduces tension between us and God that can undermine our faith and trust in a loving Father in Heaven. Puzzled by what God is "doing to us," we lose confidence in ourselves, faith in God's wisdom, and our sense of purpose in life. This idea is simply not true.

There are at least four basic causes for the various troubles we encounter in mortality and four reasons they exist.

1. Telestial Trials

We are born into a world in which opposition is built into every experience. Accidents, genetic defects, tragic acts of nature, illness, and death are inevitable in such an environment. When we drive down the freeway at breakneck speeds with thousands of other people, many texting or reading the morning newspaper, we will inevitably encounter skirmishes, and some will be deadly. Countless things happen in this telestial world without any divine intervention or involvement. These occurrences are a natural consequence of living in a fallen world around fallen mortals. Various and sundry challenges strike us all, including innocent children, righteous adults, and even God's prophets. Some things just happen, and the sooner we accept this, the less angst we will feel when these kinds of trials occur. Brooding endlessly about what God is trying to teach us at such times only leads to further confusion.

A faithful friend has an infant granddaughter who was born with several serious birth defects. After multiple surgeries and terrifying trips to the emergency room, we were talking about this difficult experience for him and his family. "These things just happen," he explained. "It's all part of the experience." Think of the unnecessary mental tension and emotional pain he has avoided by this simple conclusion.

2. Trials Caused by Others

Some of our deepest trials in mortality are caused by the actions of others. Innocent children raised by cruel and abusive parents are weighed down with emotional burdens throughout much of their lives because of their early experiences. Some children are born to drug abusing parents, who pass their terrible addiction on to their children. Many of these children can never fully overcome this addiction. These kinds of trials occur through no fault of our own but take their awful toll nonetheless. The landscape of human history is littered with broken lives at the hands of cruel oppressors, and at times these oppressors are inside our own homes, schools, neighborhoods, and families. As heinous and damaging as these experiences can be, we will see in the pages that follow that even these events can be transformed into learning experiences rather than serving as lifelong stumbling blocks.

3. Self-Inflicted Trials

More often than we realize, we bring all manner of affliction upon ourselves by our own foolishness, stupidity, naiveté, and the way we think about and react to life's difficult circumstances. While we have each been given agency to choose "according to our own desires," some of our choices are self-defeating and highly counterproductive. In my experience, these kinds of trials represent the vast majority of our greatest challenges. Rarely does God need to introduce trials into our lives. We are perfectly capable of generating plenty on our own. The ways we think, explain, and respond to everyday events often bring a host of stressful feelings that we could have completely avoided if we knew how. My own experience reveals that in the vast majority of cases, we are our own worst enemies.

4. Trials from God

Believe it or not, very few of life's difficulties and severe trials are sent to us by God. Examples of when God deliberately intervenes are so uncommon that they usually make scriptural headlines. Recall Alma and his people, who were not delivered by God from their afflictions as they so fervently prayed. The record states, "Nevertheless, the Lord seeth fit to chasten his people; yea, He trieth their patience and their faith" (Mosiah 23:21).

Many of us mistakenly conclude that God not only brings upon us our sore trials but then refuses to deliver us because He is trying to teach us something. In most cases this is neither true nor helpful. When we believe God is deliberately trying us, we far too often "charge God foolishly" (Job 1:22). In most situations we have no idea why we are passing through our present deprivations. Wanting to believe our troubles have a deep and divine purpose, we give God the credit for our woes. To think that God is behind the majority of our difficulties and trials gives God far too much responsibility for our personal trials.

When encountering a stern trial it's understandable for us to hope that God is behind it and that He has some grand design in mind that we aren't yet aware of. But when we believe that He *causes* our trials, it's a dangerously short step to believing that He wants us to suffer, which He does not.

Whether we realize it or not, when setbacks come, we immediately begin to generate possible reasons for our challenges. We like things to make sense, and we seek to explain our difficulties in a way that makes us feel better about what's happened. But what if we're wrong? What if we unwittingly create our own mess and then blame friends, parents, Church leaders, or even the Lord for what we feel required to endure? Think of the negative fallout of assigning cause to the wrong person or event. Much of what we will discuss in the pages ahead is learning what lies in our control and what does not. Coming to see our difficulties clearly is essential to responding with wisdom and avoiding a host of negative emotions brought on by seeing ourselves and our circumstances falsely.

The Savior taught, "The truth shall make you free" (John 8:32). This certainly includes freedom from error and false perception. Seeing our life situation in distorted ways makes it nearly impossible to respond to it effectively.

Much of our emotional and mental suffering is completely optional. I'm not talking about physical pain, which is rarely optional; I'm referring to the emotional pain caused by our own stressful negative emotions that accompany life's trials, setbacks, and surprises. As you read, you will discover that you have far more power over your challenges than you thought. You will learn to see things in new ways and thereby transform your dismal trials into promising opportunities. Through it all, you will learn to tap into a dimension of individual agency that often remains dormant as we labor under the weight and pressure of our lives.

Eternal truths teach us we are not here to suffer but to grow and learn. Happiness, not pain and sorrow, is the object and design of our existence.

Heavenly Father did not send us here to fail, lose hope, and shuffle off discouraged and helpless against the fierce winds of opposition. Once we learn to reclaim our power to see and respond to life's challenges in new ways, we can transform our setbacks and negative surprises into stepping stones and our burdensome feelings into stunning new insights. You will learn how to free yourself from distorted thoughts and toxic emotions, which so often accompany mortal trials, setbacks, and surprises. The truths in this book can lift your heart and mind when you are downcast and in despair. Extraordinary truths can be the springboard to extraordinary breakthroughs, and such breakthroughs increase our capacity for joy as we come to see things as they really are and as they really can be.

Notes

1. Brigham Young, *Deseret News Weekly*, 24 August 1854, 83; as quoted in L. Aldin Porter, "'But We Heeded Them Not,'" *Ensign*, Apr. 1999, 31.

THE VOICE IN YOUR HEAD

Recently, I was scanning my bookshelf for a specific book I needed for some research. When I couldn't find it, I began rifling through the stacks and pulled out an old book entitled *What You Say When You Talk to Yourself.*

That's a strange title, I said to myself. *Nobody talks to themselves—at least not normal people.* I replaced the book but then pulled it out again for a second look. I thought further about the title. *Maybe some people really do talk to themselves,* I mused. *But they don't know what they're doing. They don't realize that they are talking out loud to themselves.* The book went back on the shelf, and I returned to my search. Then it hit me. While reading and thinking about a book on talking to yourself, I had in fact been doing exactly that. I hadn't been talking out loud, but inside my head a conversation had taken place, every bit as real as if I had been talking out loud to another person in my office. For several minutes I had carried on a dialogue with myself, all within the walls of my own mind.

That night I discovered, much to my irritation, that I couldn't fall asleep. A news report kept replaying in my head and I couldn't get it to stop. I was also thinking ahead to a presentation the next morning, and that too wouldn't leave me alone. As I lay there tossing and turning, trying to shut my brain off, I grew more and more frustrated.

What's going on here? I said to myself in utter frustration. *I have to get my sleep for this meeting in the morning.* My mind was racing, darting from one subject to another. Thoughts popped into my head out of nowhere, and try as I might, I couldn't shut my brain off. Finally, I resorted to a sleeping pill, often the only weapon powerful enough to shut down the chaotic voices running through my head.

I recall the precise moment when I learned about this strange voice in my head. I was in a seminar when the teacher said, "Whether we realize it or not, all of us have a voice in our heads. It runs constantly and is largely outside our control. It is involuntary, compulsive, and never shuts up. Try as you may, you will never discover an 'off' button." I was intrigued but wondered where he was going with this bizarre idea. The speaker continued, "The voice in your head is the voice you hear right now, and it's saying something like, 'What's this guy talking about? I don't have a voice in my head. I don't hear voices. This guy is crazy.'

"Now be honest," he said. "When I say you have a voice in your head, don't you hear a voice debating this radical idea, even though you're not saying a word out loud?" Nervous laughter rippled around the room. We all realized we'd been caught. The voices in our heads were saying, *I don't have a voice in my head. Don't try to tell me that I talk to myself like I'm talking to myself right now.*

What is this curious voice that runs constantly through our minds? Where does it come from? Who is behind it, and how does it affect our lives for good or ill? What is the connection between this internal chatter and the way we think about our difficult experiences? Is it possible that understanding this inner dialogue is the key to making more sense of our trials, setbacks, and negative surprises?

Pause for a moment, right now, and notice the things running through your head. To notice the voice in your head, you must make a deliberate effort to sit back and just listen to what's happening in there. Pay close attention and you'll notice that you are not thinking, at least not consciously. Thoughts appear out of nowhere, but it is not you generating those thoughts. Instead an automatic thought-generator is at work, which you can do little about. The voice in your head runs on its own power whether you like it or not. Strange as it sounds, this voice inside your head runs constantly, day and night, and you can do very little, if anything, to stop it. Continue to watch the thinker inside your head and you'll discover that you are not these thoughts. You can step back from this constantly running stream of random and chaotic flashes of thought, as a curious bystander might observe another's conversation. But this inner dialogue is happening between your ears, right now, ten minutes from now, and often in the middle of the night when you can't get to sleep because the voice in your head is keeping you awake. If you could control the voice in your head, night time would be the time to shut it off, turn down the volume, or tell it to go away so you can get your needed rest. But the voice chatters along, even commenting on your feeble and unsuccessful efforts to shut it down.

Even though it seems that you and your voice are the same, you are not. You and your voice are separate entities. As you observe your thoughts you'll notice, *There's the voice, and here I am listening to the voice.* You are the watcher or observer of the thinker inside your head.[1] The fact that you can step back from this incessant inner commentary proves that you are not that voice and you are not in charge of what it says or when it speaks. Your mind has a mind of its own. It's a voice that is constantly commenting, judging, musing, questioning, explaining, interpreting, agreeing, disagreeing, and planning, to name just a few things.

Once you begin to notice the voice in your head, you'll realize that you're never alone. The voice is always there. You've always got your thoughts, wherever you go, whatever you do. It is running when you wake in the morning, wearies you during breakfast, stresses you out during rush-hour traffic, and goes with you to work. There, it comments on other people, judges what they say, explains what's happening in a meeting, and even interprets the boss's troubling comments on possible downsizings in the coming weeks. You hear the word *downsizing*, and the voice in your head races headlong into the future. Before you know it, you are dragged along by a strong and unrelenting current of stressful, fearful, and anxious thoughts. But remember, this is not *you* generating these thoughts, nor are these thoughts true just because you think them. Thoughts arise from nowhere like mental bubbles. When we choose to believe, attach ourselves to, or allow ourselves to be swept along by stressful and negative thoughts, we lose control. At such times we no longer choose, create, and live our lives according to our own desires. We hand the steering wheel of life over to the powerful voices in our heads, which often do not have our best interests in mind.

All of us long for peace. Perhaps this includes time when we're not assaulted by the rushing, unrelenting stream of thoughts inside our heads. Quieting the voices in our heads, however, is easier said than done.

The mind is much like other automatic mechanisms in the body such as breathing. You don't consciously focus on taking breaths in and out, but your body, by design, will breathe nonetheless. Until oxygen grows thin, you rarely notice this constant involuntary process keeping you alive from moment to moment. You don't consciously think about digestion, hormonal releases, or the miracles of eyesight, hearing, and speech. You just see and speak with very little, if any, awareness of the process. The voice in your head is equally automatic, compulsive, and involuntary, and it too occurs without any effort or awareness on your part.

Making sense of life's trials and tribulations and the stressful emotions they produce requires an increased understanding of this internal voice. More than you realize, the voice in your head dictates the quality of your life and the impact difficult experiences will have on you. If you let it, that voice will define what a setback means, what to expect as a result of a difficult experience, and what a trial says about your moral status. Someone may have a stern trial and think to himself, "God has sent me this trial because I have not attended church regularly in the past year." But this is just a thought, an explanation, a theory. If he accepts this thought and believes it's true, it can generate a string of stressful, counterproductive emotions that will prevent him from getting what he really wants.

Part of the mind's job is to make sense of what happens to us. Thus the voices in our head explain and interpret events; the voices tell us what our experiences mean. These thoughts arise out of nowhere and are not statements of truth that we must automatically accept and be afflicted by. They are simply thoughts. Much of our thinking, especially our thoughts about trials, setbacks, and negative surprises, is distorted and counterproductive. We draw all kinds of conclusions and make many assumptions. But many of our most stressful thoughts, the ones that lead to burdensome feelings, are not true. Still, we believe them because we hear them in our heads.

Clearly not everything that runs through our heads is negative and stressful. But when we judge, blame, or resent others and then believe that such thoughts are true, we will unwittingly bring upon ourselves and others a predictable string of stressful thoughts and burdensome emotions. Believing something that is untrue sets in motion a turbulent and complicated internal drama.

Take Carl for instance. He owns a small business that sells home appliances. He believes that everyone he knows, especially his neighbors and friends, should patronize his store. He has no idea that he holds this belief, nor how it affects him. One night he is invited to a party at a neighbor's home where he spots a new dishwasher and microwave oven—neither one purchased from him. Without knowing it, his mind begins to spin a negative story. What follows is a rush of stressful and judgmental thoughts inside his head that greatly impacts him in many ways.

I can't believe these people, he says to himself angrily. *They know I sell home appliances like this. What kind of friends are they to buy something and not try to help me out? I thought that's what friends were for! I can't believe it. This is ridiculous.*

As with most of us, one stressful thought leads to another, like waves crashing on the shore, and the more he nurses his thoughts, the angrier he becomes. After a few minutes, he tells the host he has a headache and needs to go home, dragging his confused wife behind him. "I refuse to stay in that house another minute," he snarls. "Those people are not my friends if they can't even support me and my business."

All of this takes place inside Carl's own head. The voice in his head crafts a stressful, judgmental story that Carl believes as true. He knows nothing of the other people; he does not know their situation or reason for not purchasing from him. The stressful story spinning within Carl's head isn't interested in their reasons and excuses. There is no excuse for what they have done. According to the voice in Carl's head, he has been wronged by people who he thought were his friends and he won't stand for it.

Sometimes the voices in our heads can be our worst enemies but only because, in most cases, we are totally unaware that we are being led along by a fabricated mental story. We assume that the thoughts, judgments, and interpretations we make are true because if they weren't, we wouldn't think them. Had Carl had the presence of mind to notice his negative thoughts and catch himself earlier, he could have avoided all the blame, resentment, anger, and subsequent separation that he created between him and his "disloyal" neighbor.

Stressful thoughts like Carl's arise quickly in the mind when life goes differently than we expect. The voice in your head is strong and forceful, and you experience it as the "truth" of what is happening to you. But if negative and stressful feelings accompany your thoughts, that tells you that you are embracing a lie. The truth will never leave you with stressful, negative feelings like those that afflicted Carl. He thought his neighbors caused his anger by failing to buy from him. They were at fault, and he did nothing wrong. If you blindly follow the voice in your head, and if that voice is judgmental and accusatory, your negative emotions will narrow your view of the situation. Carl could see nothing but his insensitive neighbors' actions because he was blind to his own stressful reaction. This neighbor did not cause Carl's negative reaction. All his neighbor did was buy a microwave and dishwasher. Everything after that played out inside Carl's mind as the voice in his head led him down a highly stressful and self-defeating path.

You may read this story and think, *That's ridiculous. Carl is childish and immature to react like that. I would never do such a silly thing.* But who thinks Carl is childish? The voice in your head judged Carl just as effortlessly as Carl judged his neighbor. And you were no more aware of your judgment than Carl was. Such is the nature of the automatic, involuntary, and often sinister voice in your head that so easily interferes with your peace and joy.

Some have said that it is a dreadful thing not to be able to stop thinking, but dreadful or not, none of us are able to stop thinking entirely. What is actually dreadful and often self-defeating is our total lack of awareness of the stressful thoughts that dominate our minds and their effect on our feelings and actions. Toxic thoughts are harmful because we wholeheartedly believe them. Think how differently life might be for us if when negative and self-defeating thoughts arose, we could simply notice them as a curious observer. As we did, we would recognize that we are not the voices in our heads. We are the observers of what our minds are thinking.

We intuitively understand the powerful influence that our thoughts can have on the quality of our lives, especially when those thoughts are negative and stressful. For instance, we hear what other people say and can easily tell when their negative thoughts are getting in their way. Even though this is so easy to see in others, we are hard-pressed to observe similar negative patterns in our own thinking. But our lack of awareness of what's running through our heads enables the voices and the stressful stories they generate to run our lives—often down very stressful paths. What we say when we talk to ourselves and how we relate to what we say determines the quality of our lives and all our relationships, as Carl's sad story illustrates. Therefore, if we're unaware of what's running through our heads and are clueless of the impact of believing our thoughts, we surrender our will to the strong current of stressful thinking.

The voice in your head is simply an ongoing conversation with yourself. A close friend recently shared a conversation she had with herself that beautifully illustrates the power of an increased awareness of this inner dialogue. She and her husband have had a difficult time having children after several years of marriage. Not long ago, her doctor reminded her that some couples go through costly procedures and still cannot have children. As she drove home, she started thinking further on what the doctor had said. Soon she was on the verge of tears as the possibility of never having children mushroomed from a single thought to a terrible eventuality. The more she thought about this horrible outcome, the worse she felt. And the worse she felt, the more probable seemed the possibility. Then suddenly she had a moment of clarity. For the first time she became the observer of her own stressful mind. She became aware of the stream of stressful thoughts running through her head, creating her strong negative and fearful feelings.

In that moment of clarity, she deliberately noticed what she was thinking and what her thoughts were making her feel. An increased awareness can break the spell that overtakes us when we feel swamped by stressful thoughts we believe are true. She began to analyze her thoughts and her reaction to what the doctor had said.

That's something this doctor knows little about, she said to herself, disputing the stressful thoughts she was having. *How does he know what will happen to me just because it has happened to others? He has no idea if this is true for us, and I'm not going to let it drag me down. Nobody knows what will happen, and I get to decide how I will react to what he said.* Her awareness set her free from the prison of dark feelings that such stressful thoughts produce.

In that split second, she cut off a stressful string of thoughts that could have left her depressed and discouraged for days as she ruminated on it. Instead she observed the thought, noticed how it was affecting her, and disputed what she was thinking, replacing it with another thought that was every bit as valid as the one the well-intended doctor had introduced. Becoming aware of the voices in our heads holds that kind of power and transforming possibility for all of us.

"It's amazing," she told me later, "how our minds spin off in some direction that can make you crazy. Then you realize, it's just a thought, nothing more, and either I can succumb to it or question it, refute it, and replace it with a different thought." Think about how much emotional turmoil we could avoid if we could develop the capacity to notice, refute, and replace stressful thoughts when they arise.

What was the real difference between angry Carl and this insightful woman? One simple thing made all the difference: my friend became aware of the stressful thoughts running through her head, while Carl was completely swallowed up by them. She used her awareness to separate herself from her thoughts and instead used her mind for a productive purpose. Carl's mind, and the negative story it spun, ran the show for Carl. He wasn't using his mind. In a very real sense, it was using him.

Since stressful thoughts produce stressful emotions, our feelings provide a critical clue for us if we can learn to notice how we feel. Negative feelings always signal to us that there is something twisted, distorted, or utterly flawed in our thinking. As the mind interprets, judges, and assigns blame and responsibility, certain feelings will arise. Paying attention to negative feelings tells us that we need to look inside, examine our thoughts, and be the observers of the thinkers inside our heads. This is something few of us ever do. Noticing is not hard if we simply let our feelings direct us to engage in quiet reflection on the stressful stuff running through our heads. This is the first critical step to making sense of life's stern experiences. While many of our challenges arise through no fault of our own, how we think about and react to these experiences is significant.

Thus our stressful feelings are always a function of our thoughts and beliefs. For example, if a student does poorly on an important test, what he thinks about his grade and what he thinks it means will forecast his emotional future, at least in the short term. Unchecked, however, a single negative thought, accepted as true, can set in motion a series of events that alters major career decisions.

As you begin noticing the voice, you'll also notice that by watching your mind, you loosen its grip over you. The voice gets its power only by remaining in the darkness of your unconscious mind. Shine the light of awareness on it, and it loses its power. Thus, the voice in your head and its various expressions derive power from your complete lack of awareness of its existence. We naturally assume that if we think something, it is true, even when that thought generates stressful feelings within us.

Ironically, our feelings are used as proof that we are thinking correctly. We tell ourselves, "I wouldn't feel this way if it wasn't true." But in fact, our feelings flow from whatever we believe to be true. When it comes to our feelings, whether or not the thoughts running through our heads are actually true matters very little. If we believe what we think is true, these thoughts will produce matching negative emotions.

When the voice in your head is negative and judgmental, it begins to feed on itself. Often, one stressful thought snowballs into another, and before long you are overcome with a headful of distressing thoughts you believe are true.

Much of what causes us to suffer, those things we label as trials or intense challenges, arise out of our complete lack of awareness of the voices in our heads and the power they have over us. That's why noticing the voice is crucial to avoiding the negative emotional fallout that flows from a single stressful thought as we think about it for days on end, never pausing long enough to reflect on the voice and its impact on us, emotionally and spiritually. It is our ignorance of what's happening inside our heads that gives the voice so much power over us.

THREE STEPS TO FREEDOM

How do we gain some measure of freedom from the persistent and often stressful voices in our heads? First, a reminder: the voice in your head and the automatic, often stressful, thoughts it generates derive their power from your lack of awareness. The moment you cast the light of awareness upon them, they lose their grip over you. They are brought into the open where you can see them and examine them. Whenever you hold onto untrue thoughts, you will experience negative feelings. Thus, the focus of this three-part investigation is on truth. You must learn to ask yourself the following questions: Is this stressful thought really true? Can I know for certain that it's true? Through this process you will take on the role of a private investigator, reviewing certain bits of information to determine if the evidence is sound and valid. You will learn to establish the truth. This is done in three relatively easy steps:

Notice Stressful Thoughts

It's important to realize that we are not our thoughts. This is a huge breakthrough for many people. They assume their thoughts are a given and that if a thought appears, it must be true. "After all," we reason, "why would I entertain ideas, opinions, and judgments that are untrue and flawed?" Strange as it may seem, we do it constantly with no regard to what we are thinking or its impact on our feelings and actions. In many ways, the voices in our heads are the engines that drive our lives for good or ill. Therefore, the more aware we can become of what's going on between our ears, the more power we can exert over self-defeating, counterproductive thoughts that do not serve us well. The first step is to notice.

The easiest way to do this is to simply become more mindful of what's running through your head. Take a few minutes and simply notice what's darting about inside your head. You'll discover a strange, often chaotic, inner-dialogue that runs on and on without your involvement and usually without your awareness—and that's the problem. You'll discover that your mind seems to have a mind of its own, separate from you. You'll see that you are not your thoughts. The very fact that you can step back from this incessant stream of thought and notice it proves that you are much more than the voice in your head. It's helpful to do this in times of relative calm when you can easily notice. Go for a walk and simply pay attention. Listen with an ear of awareness. Notice the sights, sounds, and smells all about you. Notice your breath as it flows in and out of your body. Just pay attention to what you typically don't even notice. The moment you realize that you are not your stressful thoughts, you gain power over them and they lose their power over you. Take time, at several intervals during the day, to pause and simply observe your mind at work. It's a fascinating and revealing exercise. It requires no doing, just being more aware, more mindful. Generally we are caught up by the content of our mind and fall under its spell. Stepping back and noticing our minds spinning away, doing what they do, helps us break the spell.

Inquire

Because we are largely unaware of what runs through our minds, we are easily swallowed up by our stressful thoughts. To observe the stream of thoughts is a critical first step. Likely you'll notice that the voice in your head is very judgmental. That voice is constantly agreeing, disagreeing, or offering opinions about what's right or wrong, good or bad—what you should or shouldn't do. Many of these thoughts, judgments, or stories are negative and stressful. But are they really true? That's the primary question, and it's one we rarely ask.

For example, a good friend recently lost his job. Immediately he sunk into dark thoughts of despair, intense financial worries, and questions of self-worth. His dominant thoughts were, "I'll never find a job in this economy. I'm too old, too overqualified, all washed up before my time." If such thoughts flooded your mind, what kinds of feelings do you think would follow? Stressful thoughts always generate stressful feelings, and this man was overcome with fear, dread, and despondency. This was no surprise. As he glumly shared this depressing story with me, I simply asked, "Is it true?"

He stared at me with a puzzled look. "What do you mean?" he asked.

"Well, you've told me that you think you'll never find work again, that you're all washed up and will suffer great financial setbacks. These are the thoughts that dominate your mind right now. I'm simply asking you to step back, look at these thoughts, and ask a simple but important question. For each of your thoughts ask, is it true? Can you really know for certain that it's true?"

Once more he looked at me as if I were from another planet and said, "I'm not sure what you're getting at."

"It may seem strange, John," I continued, "but it's helpful to think about your current thoughts as simply one set of thoughts out of hundreds of possible thoughts. Someone else could lose his job and have a different reaction, hold different thoughts, and hear a different story inside his head. Regardless of what you're thinking, it's clear that your current thoughts aren't serving you well. Is it possible that despite what you believe, these thoughts may not be true? That's all I'm suggesting."

"They sure seem true," he said without much reflection.

"I'm sure they seem true, and clearly they feel true, but that's not what I'm asking you to think about. Look at the thought, 'I'll never find work again.' Can you know with absolute certainty that this very stressful thought is true? Can you really know that, John?"

"Well, I suppose not," he answered.

"But look at how you react, how you feel and behave when you believe this thought is true. Can you see what happens when you merely accept such thoughts without inquiring into their veracity? Can you see where it leads?"

"I'm starting to get the picture," he said, brightening.

This is the picture we must all focus on when engulfed by stressful feelings. These feelings originate in thoughts or clusters of thoughts that our minds weave into stories, often very stressful stories. Since we rarely think about our thinking, we assume these stressful stories are absolutely true, when in fact they are just stories that we must investigate in order to find the truth. Questioning the validity of what we hear inside our heads may appear strange, but that's only because we're not accustomed to being fully aware of our thinking. Never is this more critical than when the voices in our heads are awash with troublesome, negative things.

Reframe

Through honest inquiry, we learn that what we accept wholly as true usually is not true at all. Reframing is a process of substituting different, more positive thoughts for the negative and stressful thoughts that occupy our minds. In essence, we're "trying on" various thoughts and inquiring into them.

With John, I suggested he try on the opposite of what he was thinking—something like, "I will find work again. I am not washed up, and things will work out in time." I asked him to write these new thoughts on a piece of paper so that we could consider them.

"Now, John," I continued, "let me ask you a couple questions about these thoughts. Are they as true as or perhaps even truer than your original negative thoughts?"

He looked pensively at the paper where he had written these new statements.

"Remember, John, this is simply another way to think about what recently happened with your job. You can think about it any way you choose, but your most natural and automatic thoughts have left you an emotional wreck. You can't sleep, you've lost twenty pounds, you're worried sick, and you're dealing with stomach ulcers and other unwanted consequences. And why? Because you have a story running through your head that you believe is true. This is a dark, dismal story in which you are a pathetic unemployed man with no positive future. You think this story is true. That's why you're so afflicted by it. And that's why I asked you if you can know for certain that what you think and believe is really true.

"I'm asking you to consider a different line of thought, tell a different story that might be just as true and will be far less stressful. You told me that you can't really know if your stressful story is true. So look at a very different string of thoughts about the same event. Are these more promising and optimistic thoughts as true as or truer than the thoughts that brought you down?"

"Yes," John replied, "I think they are just as true. I can't know for sure, but they seem just as true as what I've been thinking. They certainly feel a lot better."

"And how does it make you feel when you think that a more optimistic story might be just as valid as the terribly depressing story you currently believe?

"Well," he said, "clearly I've got to find different ways to think about what has happened. What I'm doing now is killing me."

This was essentially what I was asking him to do and what I'm asking you to do now. Think differently and see how that makes you feel. Try on a different explanation and see if it isn't as valid as the story that's destroying your peace. Challenge the story you now believe, and see if it's actually true. Most of us don't even know that we have the ability or power to have such conversations with ourselves, but we can.

Refuting and reframing the story that afflicts us is not just simplistic positive thinking. Rather, it is a proven process based on proven behavioral science. Stressful feelings originate in stressful thoughts that we believe are true. Since we can't *know* if they are true, we're totally engulfed by a simple belief and acceptance of what we *think* is true. Thinking *I'm all washed up and I'll never find work again* doesn't make it so, but believing these thoughts floods our souls with a host of negative emotions that immobilize us. The way out of this conundrum is surprisingly easy yet powerful. We simply consider alternative ways of thinking that are less stressful. In so doing we learn that, far more than we realize, we are dragged along by stressful thoughts, judgments, and stories we can't even know are true. But because we accept them as true, we behave and feel as if they are true.

Learning about the automatic, ceaseless, and stressful voice in your head can change your life. Never again will you feel like a helpless victim of your runaway thoughts. You will come to understand that thoughts are just things—and things can change. Thoughts are not true unless we accept them as true, and even believing they're true doesn't make them so. Think of the emotional fallout of accepting a stressful thought or series of thoughts as true. Conversely by learning to notice, inquire, and then reframe our stressful thoughts, we exercise a dimension of individual agency that we didn't even know we possessed. Only a lack of awareness empowers the stressful mind and its self-defeating voice to exercise any power over us. Therefore, becoming mindful is the solution to this curious challenge.

Notes

1. Eckhart Tolle, *Practicing the Power of Now: Essential Teachings, Meditations, and Exercises from The Power of Now* (Novato, California: New World Library Audio, 2003), book on CD. See also Eckhart Tolle, *The Power of Now* (Novato, California: New World Library, 1999).

Telling Stories

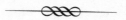

When my kids were little they loved it when I told them bedtime stories. My blindness prevented me from being able to read storybooks like other parents, so I made up my own. They featured Grandpa Moses and his friend Toby the Bear. These two characters had a variety of other friends like two horses—Silverwing and Flicka—Carla the cow, Milton the muskrat, and others. After a while, these stories became the primary tactic my wife and I used to get our kids to settle down and get into bed.

"If you don't get your teeth brushed and get your jammies on, you're not getting a Toby story," we threatened at least ten thousand times. Soon our kids were so addicted to Toby stories that when I was out of town on business I was forced to record several Toby stories for my wife to play for the kids in order to get them to cooperate at bedtime. Initially, I thought I was doing this for my kids, but my wife informed me that it was mostly for her since the kids were much easier to handle when they had the prospect of a Toby story to look forward to.

Twenty years later, I'm still telling stories, and so are you. Some of the stories we invent are harmless enough. Others can get us into places we don't want to be and make us miserable by bringing various taxing trials upon us. In this chapter you will read one such stressful story that I lived through several years ago. The key point in this story is determining if it's true or made up, like my old Toby stories. I recall my kids asking me quite often, after I told an exceptional Toby story, if the story was true or if I had made it up.

"Did Toby and Grandpa really travel to another planet where everything was made of chocolate?" they asked wide-eyed when they were supposed to have tired eyes. Usually I would say something like, "Of course it's true. Do you think I would make something like that up? Maybe one day, if you're really good, we can go there. Now go to sleep."

In a volume dedicated to making sense of what troubles us, especially our stressful trials and difficult experiences, understanding the stories we tell is key. Often, the reason for our suffering is in the story we tell about our experiences, not the experience itself. To make sense of life's difficulties, we need to pay special attention to these stressful stories we tell, like the one I'm about to relate.

Several years ago, out of the blue, I found myself embroiled in a nasty lawsuit with a former friend and colleague. He hired aggressive "pit bull" attorneys who were out for blood, and the more the better. Never in my life had I dealt with such people. They seemed to take delight in intimidating me with the possibility of losing everything I had. Another attorney, familiar with such aggressive tricks, advised me to fight back with full force. Short of any better advice, and feeling terribly vulnerable, I enlisted my attorney to enter the ring for a nine-month brawl with the pit bulls.

Notice that in every story we tell, there are two parts. First, there are the basic, fundamental facts, and then there is the story we tell about the facts. Usually these are fused into a single experience, and we lose sight of how and why we are twisting the facts into our version of what happened. The facts are those things that a video camera could capture. A story told with only the facts would go like this: "The phone rang. He picked it up, sat back in his chair, and stared out his window. Then he sat down at his computer and started typing." The stories we tell include much more than the basic facts; they include everything else that colors the facts, our thoughts, interpretations, judgments, reactions, assignments of blame, feelings, and so on. Yet the facts remain, beneath our interpretations of judgment and pain. Facts carry with them no emotion or meaning. In every invented story, the facts are meaning*less* until we make them meaning*ful* by the stories we tell.

It's easy to see how much opinion, judgment, and creative interpretation goes into the stories we spin—especially those that revolve around a setback or negative surprise. Our minds do this so effortlessly and automatically that we barely notice it. At the first sign of a setback, disappointment, or negative surprise, our minds set to work explaining the trial, making it meaningful by tossing out likely interpretations of its purpose. Usually the experience and our story about the experience are so tightly interwoven that we don't even experience them as separate things.

When I told family and friends my story about the nasty attorneys, I felt like I was telling them the truth. I wasn't telling a story but just sharing what happened. If anyone had said, "Interesting story, Randy," I would have said, "What do you mean, interesting story? This isn't just a story—it's the truth." Woven into our stories are levels of meaning and translation of the facts and events. For instance, part of my story included what seemed to me a fair judgment of my colleague as a hypocrite. My story also included how wrong he was and how it could have all been prevented if my associate would have simply had the decency to call me up and talk it over. Blame, resentment, labeling, judging, and justification were all woven tightly into my story about this ridiculous and completely unnecessary lawsuit. My story conveniently cast me as an innocent victim of a couple of nasty attorneys and an insensitive and two-faced *former* friend. Most of our stressful stories have a victim and a victimizer, and almost always we assume the victim role. We'll see why shortly.

As is often the case, the facts of this experience included none of the additional meaning my story provided. Think how colorless, and indeed meaningless, the basic facts would have sounded. "An attorney called to tell me that an old colleague was suing me. I decided to hire an attorney and see what happened." Certainly there's nothing in the facts to produce a wrenching emotional bombshell in my life. Facts are just facts with no substantive meaning. But the story we invent about the facts and what they mean can be the source of tremendous emotional pain. This was true for me.

As the days dragged by, the impact of this painful experience began to take its toll. I couldn't sleep, lost all interest in food and life, started taking anti-depressants, and more than once wondered if this experience would destroy me. What I couldn't see was already killing me.

My blindness to the truth was the underlying source of my emotional burdens. This intense pressure didn't arise from the facts but from the story I told about the facts. It came from what I had made the facts mean. As I have already said, we are not disturbed, troubled, stressed out, and anxious because of what happens to us, but because of our thoughts (including our interpretations and stories) about what happens. But caught up in the middle of such an experience, we are barely able to function, much less analyze our thoughts. Such is the power of strong negative emotions to override our ability to think clearly and act with wisdom in our own best interests.

After months of legal posturing, sword rattling, and innumerable threats, the fiasco ended, and so did this sad story—or did it? It has been said that old stories never die but are buried alive, only to come out later in uglier ways. At the time I assumed that once the legal battle officially ended so would my stress and my other stress-related symptoms. That wasn't true. For months afterward, I licked my wounds but couldn't seem to pull out of the dark hole into which this experience had cast me. Everything was a grim reminder of the money spent, the physical and emotional fallout that persisted, and the protracted pain of such a wrenching experience. Friends reassured me that time would heal my wounds, so I trudged ahead as best I could, hoping that one day the cloud would lift.

Six years later I attended a seminar with a friend. The topic of the seminar was the stories we tell about our difficult life experiences. "I'd like to give you each a few quiet moments," said the instructor, "to think about a painful experience that still lives inside you, in spite of the passage of time. What story do you still tell that just won't let go of you?" The room grew quiet as we all stared at the ceiling or floor, trying to recall such an experience. The lawsuit story rushed into my mind so quickly that I was a bit taken aback. I thought to myself, *That's silly. It's been six years. I'm way past that now. I need to think of something else.* But when the five minutes were up, that was the only story that still lit me up emotionally.

We were then handed a piece of paper and asked to write out the story with as much detail as we could recall. I remembered far too many painful details to jot down on one piece of paper. I sketched out the highlights of my painful story so that it would be easy to retell. Next we were asked to turn to our neighbor and read what we had written, which I did with ease. The teacher told us that the more often we told the story in a setting like this, the more we would see the fallacy and the more it would lose its grip on us. We were instructed to move around the room and tell our story to as many people as necessary until we felt some relief. Once we experienced some emotional relief from telling and retelling the story, we could return to our seat. After thirty minutes of telling my story over and over again, I looked around and saw that everyone in the room had returned to their seats except for me. I was the last person in the room of one hundred fifty people who was still struggling with my story. I was invited to leave the room and keep telling the story until I was ready to move on. I left the large room, sat with a friend in a small room next door, and told my story to her several times, waiting, I suppose for something to change. It never did.

A therapist friend of mine was in that same workshop and saw what happened with me. The next day he called to talk about it. I felt like others in the room had only sat down because they were tired of the silly exercise. I explained to him, "I was the only truly honest one in the room, unwilling to surrender, until I noticed a real improvement."

"Well, even though I'm sure you're tired of talking about it, it might be useful to tell me the story," said my friend. "Then we can see if there's anything in there or not." Several times over the years since the lawsuit, I had met with this friend, and he had always been kind and very helpful. At times I had also wondered if there wasn't something for me to learn from this experience. And I really had been surprised that this experience had come to my mind so quickly after so many years. All I knew was that simply telling the story had not changed how I felt about the experience. I knew there was something more I was supposed to experience, but I had no idea how to uncover it.

I told Robert the story much as I had told others, only this time it was much more condensed. I had grown so weary of dragging myself and others through the gory details of this unfortunate experience. My extensive novel of a story had been reduced to little more than a footnote. "I was sued. It ruined my life and cost me a lot of money, and now, thankfully, it's over."

"Sounds pretty innocuous," said Robert after listening to the story. "How are you feeling about it now, after telling it over and over yesterday?"

"I really don't know anymore," I admitted. "I want to think that I have moved past this dreadful experience, but it still seems to live inside me, and it still carries a load of strong emotions with it." Robert asked me how I felt about the colleague who had sued me, and I launched into my standard story about him being dishonest, duplicitous, and a tremendous hypocrite. "If he would have had the decency to just come and talk to me we could have avoided all of this," I added with finality. "This entire absurd experience accomplished nothing, and he caused it all." This was a twist on the story I had not told people at the seminar. No one had ever asked how I felt about the experience or the people who brought it about. This was where my strongest and most piercing emotion lay. I was a bit surprised that my feelings had lost no intensity over the years. This story and its effect on me still had a hold that I couldn't seem to shake. I wanted to let it go, move on, and leave it all behind me, but for some reason, I couldn't pull it off. After six long years, it still haunted me in ways I didn't really understand.

"Sounds like you're ready to see this experience in new ways and move on. Is that right?" asked Robert.

"Well," I said, sighing, "I confess that I have learned nothing from what happened except to be more cautious and wary of associates who, at any time, can stab you in the back. If you're about to ask what this has taught me, that's all I've ever gotten from this nasty experience."

Learning from our trials is not always easy. We often feel fortunate simply to have survived an experience, much less gain some profound new insight from it. And yet, isn't that the ultimate reason for such experiences? If we really take away nothing positive and learn only several negative conclusions like, "beware of your friends," the experiences leave us worse off than we were before them. I soon understood, with Robert's able assistance, how to learn important lessons from severe trials, regardless of why they occurred.

Robert asked me to describe the man who had sued me in as much detail as I wanted. That was easy. He was in every way a dishonest, two-faced hypocrite. He could have handled the situation like a man, but he chose to hide behind attorneys and legal jargon rather than face me personally. I blamed and resented him for all I had gone through because in my mind that pain could have easily been avoided.

As I freely pointed out the many sins of my former friend, Robert listened carefully. Then he asked a question that left me speechless. "Can you think of any time in your relationship with this man when you were dishonest or behaved in a hypocritical way?" In all the years since that first nasty call from an attorney, I had never reflected on my own actions. I had blamed, accused, resented, and told my story to anyone who would listen. But I had never thought seriously for one minute about anything I had said about this man. Never had I reflected on my anger, my blame, or my reaction to what he had done. My entire focus was outward—on him, on what he had done, what it said about him, and on its impact on me, my life, and career. Now Robert was asking me to turn the mirror toward myself and look for times when I had said or done the same kinds of things I so easily accused him of.

Never before had I ever focused on my part in the experience. My focus was squarely and fully on my opponent: his wrongs, his unwillingness to confront me man to man, his dishonesty and duplicity, and his acting self-righteous to the world while suing people with his pit bull attorneys behind closed doors. Now, after all these years, after all the blame, resentment, and anger that I had easily justified for so long, Robert was asking me to think about this experience in an entirely different way.

Robert's simple question nearly turned my brain inside out. He could tell I was struggling to get my head around it. "The key to your healing, Randy, lies in repenting of what you have said and done. In many ways, it has nothing to do with him or anything he has done. The reason you are still stuck is because you haven't really let go of the blame and accusation. These toxic emotions still course through your heart and mind and undermine your peace and productive learning."

When he asked if I had been dishonest, shady, or hypocritical with the man who had sued me, the hot blush of shame and guilt washed over me. As soon as he asked the question, I knew the answer. But I still resisted it. It was as if I knew the truth but was afraid of facing it. I shared what I had done before the lawsuit that had led my friend to sue me. I had been unfair, sneaky, and duplicitous. Somehow I had justified my own dishonesty by blaming him. I then realized that I had accused my former friend of things I was also guilty of and then covered up my guilt with blame and finger-pointing. But, of course, having done this for years, telling and retelling the same story, I found it deeply rooted inside me as truth. I slowly began to see, as painful as it was, that before the lawsuit and all the difficult consequences that followed, I had made several serious mistakes but I'd found a way to justify it all through rationalization and resentment.

As we talked this through, the truth of the situation began to slowly dawn on me. I saw that I was still doing the very things I had accused my opponent of doing for so long. I had been less than honest and yet I'd bitterly accused him of dishonesty. I justified my own hypocrisy by focusing on his. I blamed him for blaming and suing me. Given what I had done, I realized that he did the only thing he could do under the circumstances. Never in a million years could I have seen that everything I had accused him of doing was a mirror-image reflection of my own unacceptable actions. I had unwittingly caused my own suffering for all those years. Simply put, I was finally seeing the situation honestly.

In his landmark book *Emotional Resilience*, Dr. David Viscott writes of the critical role that telling the truth had for his mental health patients. Months of intense therapy stalled out until patients were willing to tell the unvarnished truth of their life situations. But many approached the truth with great trepidation. "Approaching a concealed truth made my patients increasingly uncomfortable. They yearned to know it, but were afraid of what they would discover. It was a turning point for many of them. Some were strongly motivated by their discomfort. . . . It was as if hearing themselves lie activated the displeasure of a higher, more spiritual self within that could no longer tolerate deception."[1]

I surely felt this discomfort. After taking a defensive position for so long and telling countless people of my pathetic story, I was seeing the truth for the first time—and I didn't like what I saw. But it was clear to me that something had to be done to free me from the burdens I still carried after so many years. The lie at the center of my pain finally became evident. I had blamed all my misery, emotional turmoil, and mental strain on this man and the lawsuit I felt he'd unjustly initiated. I had been unwilling to accept any responsibility and believed I had done nothing wrong. That was a lie and that lie and the defensiveness that surrounded it now came painfully into focus. As I talked through this entire experience with Robert, holding back nothing, the truth began to surface, and the darkness of deception gave way to the light of insight and the clarity that truth always brings.

The more we talked, the clearer it all became. Finally, after the years of anger, bitterness, blame, and resentment, I saw and accepted the *real* truth that I had vigorously resisted for so long. Still, I wasn't sure what to do about something that had taken place nearly seven years earlier.

"Robert," I said with some uncertainty, "how do I fix what I have done? What can I do after all this time?"

"There are two ways you can handle it," he explained. "Either write him a letter and lay this all out for him as you have for me, or go visit him and talk it over. Talking to him personally may be more difficult, but it may also be a lot more therapeutic for both of you." As soon as Robert laid out my options, I knew what I needed to do. A letter would not be the way to go. I needed to call him up, sit down, and have an open, honest, heart-to-heart conversation.

After some coaching from Robert about how to handle this delicate and important conversation, I picked up the phone and made the call. Though nervous about how the other man might react, I knew I was doing the right thing by dealing with this scorching experience.

The phone rang and soon I heard his voice on the line. "I know it's been a long time since we've talked," I began slowly. "I've been doing a lot of thinking about what's happened between us. I now see that I have done a lot of foolish things. Would you be willing to meet with me sometime and talk things over?"

"Absolutely," he said brightly. "When would you like to meet?" A time was set for three days later. I got off the phone a bit surprised by two things: first, how willing he was to meet after all the bad blood between us, and second, the tension and worry that lifted immediately after the phone call. It was so perceptible, such a strong confirmation that I was on the right track and doing the right thing.

Three days later I sat outside the building where his office was located. Such a strange feeling came over me. For nearly seven years, I had maligned and resented this man, charging him for so many things in my life that had gone wrong. And now I was about to meet with him face-to-face and acknowledge the lies I had told and the part I had played in causing the lawsuit in the first place. I was struck by how easily I—a grown man, educated and committed to gospel principles—had deceived and taken in by a lie. My blaming and harsh judgment of this man had come so naturally and easily that somehow it didn't feel wrong. I hadn't felt as though I were violating any gospel principles. A part of me I didn't like had taken delight in making him wrong and justifying my own mistreatment of him. This seems to be the challenge that we all face when engulfed by intense negative emotions brought on by a misunderstanding or a falling out with another person. It is truly amazing what we justify and explain away as we engage in the very things we resent others for doing to us.

A few minutes later, he ushered me into his office. He sat down and waited patiently for me to speak.

"Thank you for taking time to meet with me," I said, a bit uncertain about how to begin. "I'm sorry if I stumble around a bit. I've had several major insights about myself in the past few days that I'm still trying to understand. The thing I want to do first is apologize. I'm sorry for all I did to you. I now see that my own actions put you in a position where you had very few options but to pursue legal grounds. That must have been very expensive and distasteful for you. It certainly cost me a lot to defend myself and must have cost you even more." He sat quietly listening to me pour out my soul. I suspect he had rarely heard anyone speak so sincerely, and certainly he hadn't expected such a speech to ever come from me.

"I now see," I continued, "that I was dishonest. I acted without integrity. I was the hypocrite. I did all the things I have charged you with for all these years, and for that too, I am sorry. You did nothing but what you felt you needed to do based on what I had done. And yet I blamed and resented you for so long. I maligned your name to anyone who cared to listen. My promise to you is that I will go back to all those people and tell them the truth. This wasn't about what you did, but about me and what I did to bring all of this about. I wish I could have seen it earlier but I couldn't. Thankfully I saw it in time and you were willing to let me try to clean up the mess I brought upon us both. Thank you for your willingness to meet."

As I continued speaking, I shared with him what I wanted to see happen in the future, but I also told him that I would understand if he couldn't fully forgive me for all I had said and done to hurt him. I told him that I hoped we could at least meet in social settings and not feel uncomfortable. I hoped that from then on we could both think of one another in a different light and try to move past this once and for all. Tears flowed freely as I acknowledged my sincere sadness for all that had happened and my hope that he could forgive me. He turned his chair and looked out the window at the nearby mountains, deep in thought. I sat quietly, feeling the power that full disclosure and acceptance of the truth can bring.

"Isn't it interesting," he said slowly, "how we get ourselves into some of the messes we do? Life is certainly an interesting experience, and I have caused my share of difficulties for myself and others."

As I wiped my eyes and thanked him for taking the time to meet, he stood up and walked around his desk. Then we embraced. With his arm around me, we walked to the door, and he said reassuringly, "Randy, know this, you have no enemy here." With that the door closed behind me, and I walked away. As I strode down the hallway, I reflected further on his final words. "You have no enemy here." For seven years, I had viewed him as my worst enemy. After all, he was the one who had started this entire mess. He was the reason my life had been turned upside down for so long and why I was stuck in an emotional hell from which I could not escape. At least, that was my story, and as your story goes, so goes your life. During all this time that I had blamed and resented him, he had gone forward with his life. Surely he'd been bruised by the experience, but he didn't feel toward me as I had felt toward him. Thus, the only enemy I'd had was the one I had made up—a fictional character in a sad story in which I was the innocent victim of a nasty man's mistreatment. Now in the light of truth, I saw it all clearly. The story, the emotion, the burdens, the blame were real, but only because I had believed in a story that turned out to be completely untrue. With the realization of the truth came the freedom I had yearned to feel for so long.

Making sense of our emotional problems and troubled relationships demands total honesty. Whenever we think other people are causing our stressful feelings, that very thought is the problem. Other people do what they do, and we react to it. Our reactions can range from empathy, on the one end, to angry resentment or blame on the other. We all know by experience that anger, blame, and resentment come naturally to the natural man (see Mosiah 3:19). Our knee-jerk reaction when we think we have been wronged is to blame others for what they have done and for how they've made us feel. Blame is our way of avoiding responsibility for any portion of our problems.

By focusing on what others have done, we justify our own mistreatment. We justify blaming, judging, and resenting others by pointing out what they said and did. But this is complete self-deception. At the very moment we think we have the stressful situation figured out, we shut the door on all our options. Blaming others makes us miserable because it leaves us helpless to change the situation. If I see myself outside of the problem, I am, by definition, outside any possible resolution. If I honestly believe I had no part in causing what afflicts me, then I can do nothing to resolve it. Thus I am stuck, miserable, and helpless—which only adds to my inner turmoil.

Most people I know are afflicted by negative feelings generated by tension in one or more relationships. These can occur at work, in our neighborhoods or churches, and sadly, even inside the walls of our own homes. Our most natural reaction is counterproductive and defensive. But we cannot take a defensive position with a person and at the same time build our relationship with him. When we grow defensive and blame others, it is because we see the situation and ourselves falsely. This distorts our perspective, blurs the truth, and leads us to think and react in incorrect ways. And in doing so, we provoke others to do the same. Before long we are caught up in a pattern we cannot possibly abandon, even though it always makes things worse.

So how do we learn to see ourselves and our difficult relationships honestly? Here are some suggestions.

1. Learn to correctly interpret negative feelings. Our negative feelings provide reliable and critical signals to us that something is awry in our thinking. We feel as we do because of how we think about our circumstances. As Gary Zukav says, "Emotions send critical signals to us about what we need to know and understand. The more important the lesson, the stronger the emotion. We misinterpret our feelings, failing to see them as the signals they really are. Imagine how you would behave differently, if you knew that all emotion, especially negative emotion, was signaling you of things you needed to investigate in your thinking?"[2] This is a powerful insight. Let your stressful, negative feelings lead you inside to investigate the incessant thoughts and stories running through your mind. Blame, resentment, and judging will always generate within us disturbing, disruptive emotions. This is why conflict and contention are so spiritually costly. The Spirit's efforts to lead us in wisdom's paths are scrambled by the noise of anger caused by blaming and judging others.

2. The Savior taught that Satan "stirreth up the hearts of men to contend with anger, one with another. Behold, this is not my doctrine" (3 Nephi 11:29–30). Negative, stressful feelings that stir us up unto contention do not come from the Lord. Considering the emotional damage done to all involved, Satan achieves a great victory over the peace and joy we seek when we

allow him to influence us in this way. Pay close attention to your feelings.

3. Notice your justification and rationalization. Validating these feelings requires twisted emotional thinking that blurs our perceptions. Others are made to appear devilish and villainous in our eyes. But we see only what we need to see to validate our story. Viewing others as cruel and unjust makes it easier to justify ourselves through blame and resentment. We *need* to see them as the bad guy, so we have someone to blame other than ourselves.

   Thus, we are unable to see ourselves and others clearly. To justify is to make the wrong things we are doing seem right. We know that blaming, judging, and resenting others is wrong and goes against everything we know about being Christlike. This means that we can't act openly mean, hostile, or judgmental without some kind of justification. Thus, the only way I can mistreat you is to focus on what you are doing to me. That's how I justify mistreating you. "I wouldn't be acting like this, but look what he has done to me!" Our emotional logic leads us to believe that someone else is making us feel and act as we do, for which we resent them. This convoluted logic is what we invent in order to feel good about behaving badly. The toxic feelings we bring upon ourselves are another clue that we are striving to avoid the truth by deflecting attention away from our own actions and onto the unacceptable behavior of someone else. When we justify, we attempt to escape responsibility. We become upset and frustrated in part because we feel helpless, which helplessness we bring upon ourselves. This feeling of helplessness is a clear and reliable signal that we are seeing and thinking falsely. After noticing your negative feelings, look for the justifying thoughts behind them. This will take you further upstream to the source of your emotional pain.

4. Always remember that lies complicate, but truth simplifies. If you are entangled in a skirmish with another person, it usually feels complicated. This was certainly true in my protracted and complicated lawsuit story, *until* I saw things honestly. Anger, blame, and resentment always complicate a relationship because they set up a complex interaction pattern of attack and defend.

You feel you are being attacked, wronged, hurt, or offended in some way and feel you must defend yourself from this attack. "What else can I do?" you ask. But as I defend myself from your attack, you view my defensiveness as blame, which provokes your defensiveness. A painful pattern is then established in which neither person feels he can change because of the other's constant attacks.

Sadly, we see patterns like this persist for years while both sides feel justified doing all kinds of mean and nasty things to the other, provoking them to do the same—and the painful pattern rolls endlessly on. If you feel you are part of a complicated painful pattern like this, one you can't do anything about, you are seeing yourself in relation to those in false ways. If a tit for tat pattern is all too familiar to you, interpret this kind of thinking for what it really is. Rather than prove that you are right and the other person is wrong—an easy conclusion to draw—look more carefully.

If you are fully honest with yourself and are sincerely interested in changing painful patterns, begin looking at yourself, not others. It is easy to see the things that other people do to cause your stressful feelings. Now walk around to the other side of the fence and view yourself honestly. What are you doing to provoke the other person's behavior? This is not about who should be blamed. It's merely an attempt to see the full truth, the wide-angle view of your entire interaction pattern with this other person.

5. Whatever you don't own, owns you. This is a profound insight that I learned from my painful legal battle. When we blame and judge others, we imply that we do not have the weaknesses or defects they obviously have. When I bitterly blamed my colleague for being a two-faced, duplicitous hypocrite, I was in effect saying, "I am none of these things. I'm above it, better than that. I would never stoop so low." Puffed up with pride, my latent faults remained hidden from my view. In a very real way, I was a prisoner to the very same negative traits I accused my opponent of having. Whatever you don't own, or whatever you reject as a potential weakness in you, stymies you and binds you down.

Here's the exercise Robert invited me to do to dispel my blindness.

a) Make a list of the primary weaknesses you see in the person with whom you have a negative relationship.

b) Ask yourself, "Have I ever displayed these same behaviors in my actions toward this other person?" If I think you are insensitive, for instance, am I not being just as insensitive by labeling and judging you? If I think you are blunt and insensitive, am I not being blunt and insensitive to tell you so?

Honestly evaluate your actions in relation to others. Look for times when you have done the same thing you accuse others of doing or blame them for doing. As you see and own these negative traits and behaviors, your resentment of others will vanish because you will share something in common with them and you will own what formerly you rejected. Taking ownership for what you think, say, and do reduces your resentment and increases your compassion. In my example, in that moment of insight when I realized I had been dishonest and a hypocrite, I was convicted by the truth and that conviction dispelled the lies I had told myself for so long. The truth must come forth or we will remain locked in painful patterns with others and continue to be weighed down by negative emotions. When we finally see the truth, we must quickly repent of our resentment before it does any more damage to our souls.

Notes

1   David Viscott, *Emotional Resilience: Simple Truths for Dealing with the Unfinished Business of Your Past* (New York: Harmony Books, 1996), 5.

2   Gary Zukav, *The Seat of the Soul*, (New York: Simon & Schuster, 1990).

KEEPING PROMISES

I promise—a simple phrase we hear all the time. Parents and children employ it a great deal to make certain things happen. A mother says to a child, "Now, Jack, I need you to clean up your toys and then come and help me feed your little brother, okay?"

Jack says, "Okay." But his mom can tell he's not really listening.

"Jack," she says, "Look at me. I need you to do this for me. Do you promise to clean up your toys and come right downstairs?"

"I promise, Mom," says Jack, dashing off to play.

Children learn about the power of promises early in life. I can't count the times when my young kids were upset with me for failing to come through as they wanted. I'd return from a business trip, and my kids would greet me at the front door to see what I had brought them. Sometimes I brought them a little trinket and sometimes I didn't. Whenever I didn't, they would cry, "Dad, you promised!" What followed was a short debate about whether I had, in fact, promised or not. For children, this is a serious issue. If you promise and then fail to keep your promise, it seems terribly unfair. Usually children cannot accept any excuse for failing to keep a promise.

"Guys," I would say, trying to explain, "I didn't promise. I said I would try to get you something if I had time, and on this trip I just didn't have time." This rarely helped. It only increased their determination to catch me in a lie. "That's not what you said, Dad," they would often cry. "You promised. We heard you say, 'I promise.'"

Promises, of one kind or another, weave their way through nearly every aspect of life. We rely on others to keep their promises, to fulfill their commitments, to do as they agreed to do. When a promise is made between two people or even two countries, something more is added to the arrangement than a casual agreement that either side can justify breaking, whether through formal contracts or a simple handshake.

Think, for instance, how often written agreements or contracts are involved in various parts of life. So many promises are reduced to a form that you sign which attests or *promises* that you will do what you said you would do, and so will the other party. International peace treaties between two countries are legal documents that each party must sign. Why? Because a signature is a formal way of saying, "I promise," or, "On behalf of the United States, I promise to abide by all the terms of this treaty."

Business people use contracts constantly to keep their customers and dealers in line. And what do they do when someone violates the contract? If a lawsuit is filed, one of the first things entered as evidence is a signed agreement or contract. We've all seen the court scenes, with the judge and jury all trying to determine if the accused is guilty or not.

"Mr. Gibbs, we have here a signed contract from you. We enter this as Exhibit 1, your honor. Now, Mr. Gibbs, take a look at the signature on this contract. Is that your signature?"

"Yes, it appears to be my signature."

"Let it be entered into the record that Mr. Gibbs saw the contract and acknowledges that he in fact signed it with his own hand."

In normal language, this translates to something like, "This man signed his name. He admits to signing his name, and that means he *promised*." The rest of the proceedings then focus on determining whether Mr. Gibbs knowingly broke his promise, whether he was tricked into signing, or whether his accusers did something to violate their part of the promise and thereby justify Mr. Gibbs's breaking the promise. The entire stressful affair surrounds promises made and promises broken, and all the why's and wherefore's, reasons, excuses, and justifications involved.

When we promise, we literally give our word in the matter. We even use language that confirms what is involved. "I give you my word," or "You have my word." If we really want to seal the deal, we bring God into it. "As the Lord liveth," declared Nephi to his faithless brothers, "we will not go down to our father in the wilderness until we have accomplished the thing which the Lord hath commanded us" (1 Nephi 3:15). Anciently, the most solemn kind of promise one could give was through an oath. After Nephi secured the brass plates, he and his brothers held Laban's servant, Zoram, fearing that he would return to the city and tell others what had occurred. So how did they reassure one another? By each party making an oath to the other. Nephi made an oath to Zoram that if he would not escape, he would be a free man. "And it came to pass that when Zoram had made an oath unto us, our fears did cease concerning him" (1 Nephi 4:37).

This tells us of the serious nature of an oath in Nephi's time. We read this verse and wonder how their fears could cease so easily. In our day our oaths or promises mean nothing. *Of course he made an oath*, we think, *but he only promised not to run so you would trust him. Then, as soon as you turn your heads, he'll sneak off and return to the city. You can't trust people to keep their word.* But anciently, no Arab would break an oath. Their word was their bond.

This story reveals the vast difference between ancient oaths and modern casual promises. Most of us can recall several instances in our life where people have made promises and then deliberately broken them, given their word, and then turned back on it. For such individuals their word in a given situation means little. But anciently, at least in the Middle East, when a man gave his word or made an oath, he would die before breaking it. His honor was at stake.

Once someone gives us their word—either officially via a signed agreement or a verbal handshake agreement—we expect people to keep their word. When they don't keep their promises, we feel they have done something seriously wrong. "That guy told me this car had no major mechanical problems and since buying it, I've put almost two thousand dollars into it. He lied to me just so I would buy the car!" We are incensed by such deliberate manipulations of the truth. In fact, we call them lies. They didn't tell us the truth, didn't do what they said they would do, and failed to live up to their end of our agreement. We feel there is no excuse for people breaking their word. It is inexcusable.

But turn the tables and everything changes. When I break my promises to you, for example, I do so by somehow justifying my otherwise inexcusable behavior. The act of justification is a mental maneuver that involves making the wrong thing we are doing seem right or making it seem like they are certainly not our fault. There is something innate in most people that compels them to *try* to keep their promises. When we have given our word, we feel an obligation to honor our word and to do what we said we would do. But most of us break promises, fail to keep our word, and fall through on agreements all the time. Of course, we can't knowingly break our promises without offering an excuse. We must explain it, rationalize it, justify it to ourselves and others. Honoring our word seems hard-wired into our very natures. We literally cannot break a promise we have knowingly made without justifying it or in some way explaining the reason behind our broken promise. The only way we can feel good about doing bad is to justify it, rationalize it, and explain it away.

"I know I promised to love my neighbor, but he's a pompous, self-righteous jerk." In this statement, we see both the agreement to promise and the justification. The little word "but" is the mind's way of making our wrong seem right or at least not our fault. "I would be nice to my neighbor, but his behavior excuses me from doing what I would normally do."

So while we are unwilling to accept another person's lame excuse for breaking his word or openly lying to us, the first thing we do when we fail to keep our promises is to throw up all kinds of reasons, explanations, or excuses for our behavior. Oddly enough, we are irritated when others won't accept our excuses, even though we generally refuse to accept theirs. In essence we say, "There's no excuse for your behavior, but there is an excuse for mine." Therefore, while we often fail to realize it, we both agree that making and keeping promises is important. I believe you should keep yours, and you believe I should keep mine, and when either of us falls short, we immediately begin to spin reasons, rationalizations, and explanations that excuse us from doing what we know we should have done.

Why all this talk of honoring our word and maintaining integrity in a book about making sense of trials? Several important reasons: First, nothing is more personal than our word. In a very real sense, our word is all we have to offer another person. A solemn ceremony, such as a marriage ceremony, may be the most personal and important example of an occasion that involves nothing more than our word. We give our sincere promise to another person to treat them well, care for them, and behave as a married person should. This is different from saying, "I'll try my best." Instead we say to our soon-to-be spouse, "I promise to love, honor, and cherish you. I give you my word. You can count on it." This is not a casual agreement between two businessmen. Our word is placed on the line before everyone attending the service. Then, five, ten, or twenty years down the road the unthinkable happens. One spouse is unfaithful, as we call it. And to what is he unfaithful? The promise he made to himself, to his spouse, and to God to be faithful forever. Breaking these sacred vows is one of the most emotionally devastating experiences of life. Adultery is merely the tail end of a whole string of maneuvers that people engage in once they have broken their word. First comes the justification, the reasons, the excuses, and the convoluted explanations. And always there are the lies—vain and pathetic attempts to cover up the wrongs they have done. We see how people undertake all these and many more actions to try to excuse themselves from what they have done, to make their wrong-doing appear acceptable and certainly not their fault.

Behind all of this is the desperate attempt to avoid any and all responsibility. We say, "Maybe I broke my promise, but I had my reasons. I had no choice. The other person didn't do what he promised, so that justifies me doing the same. In other words, I didn't deliberately make this choice. Someone else *made* me do it." We direct the focus from our broken word to the behavior of others who "forced" us to violate our agreement.

How strongly do we feel bound to our word? Completely. Even in cases where we clearly violated our word, we *must* find a way to explain it or make it okay, given the circumstances. It's as if we say, "I know what I did was wrong, but once you hear my reasons and better understand the unique circumstances that surrounded my actions, then you'll understand that I really had no other choice. I had to do what I did." We are not saying, "I never promised." But we are saying, "I admit that I did promise, but because of extenuating circumstances, it was impossible to keep my promise."

Once you make a promise, there is only one question on the table. Will you keep the promise or not? Will you fulfill your agreement or dodge your responsibility somehow? Will you keep your agreements or break them, and then justify your actions by blaming others for failing to keep their promises?

In a sense, you and I have a relationship to our word that is either weak or strong. Those with a weak relationship to their word make promises casually, take them lightly, and break them easily. What they say and what they do are miles apart. In effect, their word means very little to them. Their promises are more mechanical, just words they say rather than a real commitment that others can rely on. We all know people like this. Whatever they say is easily dismissed, since we've learned that their word means nothing to them, whether they verbally promise, sign an agreement, or write their name in blood. They will not follow through. Their word is of little value to them.

When people fail to esteem their word highly, they end up esteeming something else. Instead of respecting their word and honoring it, they honor various reasons, excuses, and justifications. If our relationship to our word is weak, we find it easy to dishonor our word and instead honor our reasons, explanations, and excuses. We cannot honor both our word and our excuses simultaneously. If we fail to honor our word and keep our promises, we must then honor our reasons and excuses. These allow us to break our word without feeling responsible.

And what is the emotional impact of failing to honor our word and keep our promises? The more significant the promise, the more significant the impact. But there are natural, negative consequences to making a promise and then breaking it. Making promises places our individual integrity center stage. No one can make a promise for you. We each make them on our own, of our own volition. While we hear of austere parents attempting to compel their children to do certain things, it never works. Making a promise under duress is different from willfully, deliberately giving one's word to another person. Once I extend my word in a promise, I also declare my intention to behave with integrity. Whether I do what I said I would do is completely up to me. Only I can make a promise and only I can fail to keep it. This is a matter of integrity, a lining up of my word and my actions.

Since giving our word is one of the most personal and intimate things we do, failure to keep our word does not come without its emotional costs. Crafting acceptable excuses, inventing reasons, and creating various explanations for failing to keep our word can be stressful. What we're actually trying to do is justify a lie. When I say "I promise" and then fail to keep my promise, I either was unable to keep the promise or I knowingly failed to honor my word. This act brings upon me a host of negative feelings and often is the first step to interpersonal contention. The emotional energy we devote to justifying our broken promises can be draining and robs us of the peace of mind that keeping our promises always brings. Those with little esteem for their word make a mockery of personal honor. They make a promise, casually violate it, and excuse it away with ease. But look closer and you'll also see that such individuals bring upon themselves a constant string of problems. Once the value of our word dips below a certain level, life becomes chaotic and difficult. Nothing goes our way because our word easily breaks down and so do we.

RESTORING INTEGRITY

Honoring our word over excuses is not just a nice thing to do, it is the most practical strategy we have for creating a life of peace and joy. Conversely, when we consistently give in to explanations, reasons, and excuses, we can create nothing of real lasting value. In fact, when life stops working in any area, it is a clear signal that we are out of integrity—that what we have said and what we have done are failing to line up. It lets us know that somewhere, sometime we failed to honor our word or keep our agreements.

For example, if you fail to keep your promises or others fail to keep theirs, what inevitably happens? We see it so often with teenagers and their parents. Trust is lost and their words soon mean very little. They promise over and over to be home by midnight but then roll in around two in the morning with a stream of reasons and excuses, hollow attempts to blame everyone else for their broken promise. In a short time, their words, even if spoken in earnest, mean nothing. No matter what the circumstance, when trust is lost, whatever positive relationship you once had quickly begins to break down. Trust is established through honoring our words to one another, no matter who the individuals.

We are keenly aware of how other people's lack of integrity impacts us and how difficult it is to build a strong relationship with such individuals. Obviously the reverse is just as true. When we make and subsequently break our promises to others, they lose confidence in us. They struggle to trust us and are left wondering what we will really do, despite what we may say. This principle is true in any area of life. When political leaders say one thing and do another, when companies tout world-class customer service and then mistreat customers, when families lose confidence in one another for all the reasons discussed, everything breaks down. Honoring our word is not therefore merely a noble virtue as some suppose. It is the very essence of positive, long-term relationships. Without it, nothing works. When you lose it, everything else begins to shut down. Conversely, when it is a living, vibrant part of a relationship, anything is possible.

Integrity is the positive energy in life that makes everything else work. Thus, reflecting on times when we have broken promises or failed to keep important agreements can be a gold mine of answers to some of our deepest challenges. Given integrity's central role, when we see a relationship headed in the wrong direction, it is helpful to begin with our own degree of integrity to understand what lies behind the breakdown. Know this: whenever we have broken our word, for whatever reason or excuse, we will experience frustration, struggle, stress, and perhaps resignation. These are natural and predictable consequences of failing to honor our word. In ways we can't fully understand, we intuitively know that our word is all we really have. Thus when our word loses its power, it is easy for us to feel stuck and powerless.

For example consider the simple act of making a New Year's resolution to lose weight and become more fit. The holidays are over, the year is ending, and once more we look in the mirror at someone much larger and less healthy than we'd like to see. But the new year is upon us and it seems like a perfect time to set some new goals. When we set new goals, we are in effect making promises to ourselves. We even use that kind of language when we share our commitment with others. "I promised myself," we tell our spouse, "that this year I would get up an hour early and work out." Declaring what we will do is, for most, the easy part. You have given your word and made a promise or a commitment to yourself and perhaps to others. The only question now is whether you will honor your word over your excuses, reasons, and explanations.

Anyone can make a promise to others or to himself. For those with a history of flaky behavior, following through on promises is difficult. But those who say their word is their bond, will find a way to do what they said they would do. We often refer to them as serious, committed, goal-oriented individuals. But these virtues flow from honoring their word above everything else. When we fail to keep our word in areas like health and fitness, we throw out various reasons, excuses, and rationalizations for why, despite our January goal, we were simply unable to stay on track. "The weather was nasty; I was too tired in the mornings; the gym was crowded; I couldn't stay on my eating plan since we eat out so much at work." And on, and on, and on. At such times, the core issue is our failure to honor our own word over so many other reasons and excuses.

When you have a strong relationship with your word, when your word truly is your solemn bond to self and others, you honor it above every other possible explanation. This doesn't mean that you can keep every commitment you ever make. Sometimes circumstances arise that make it impossible to do what you promised to do. But if honoring your word is important to you and you understand the power that flows from it, you will immediately restore your integrity. After a slip-up on your diet, you will be back on your eating and exercise plan the next day with no flimsy explanation or pathetic excuses. This is the unlocked power of making promises, honoring those promises, and re-establishing your word.

Think of the unnecessary frustration, disappointment, stress, and resignation that results from failing to honor our word in all areas of life. As we make sense of our emotional burdens, this is one place to find juicy answers. We simply cannot break our word, violate our agreements, or flake out on our commitments without bringing upon ourselves various troublesome and stressful feelings. In any area of your life that is not working as you would like, rather than casting about for plausible excuses and reasons, ask yourself a different question: "Where have I broken my word? What agreements have I failed to keep? What promises have I not kept and to whom?"

Several years ago, I found myself in a bitter battle with one of my teenage daughters. Until she was in high school, we had always had an open, loving relationship. But when she hit seventeen, our relationship turned upside down.

She was hardheaded, stubborn, easily riled, overemotional, and disrespectful to me and her mother. Keep in mind, these were my words for describing how I saw her. These were my labels for her. I felt I had done all I possibly could to resolve our differences, but things between us went steadily downhill. We got to a point where we couldn't have a civil conversation unless it was highly superficial. She even established several conversational ground rules. "You can ask me about work and school, but I don't want to talk to you about anything else." With these clear boundaries, I would regularly ask her, "How's school and work?" and receive a standard, "Fine." This was essentially the extent of our conversations.

As you can imagine, this was difficult for me. I felt I was trying to be a concerned, loving father, but she was pushing me away. I wanted to share important things with her, but she wasn't willing to talk about them. In my mind, I had so many good intentions that went unrealized because of her. She was ruining our relationship. She was causing me to fret and ruminate over her, and even making me whine to my wife and other children about how bull-headed and ornery she was. The rest of the family agreed with me, which helped strengthen my case against her. I was innocent, and she was guilty. I honestly felt I had done everything I possibly could to reclaim her affection and trust, even though everything I said and did made matters worse.

Deeply frustrated by my daughter and determined to fix what was broken, I hired a relationship coach. In our first phone call, she even said, "I help people fix broken relationships." She went on to explain that in most cases, when a relationship isn't working, we feel we have tried everything—everything that is, but the one thing that can transform the relationship.

"I don't know what to do with this girl," I told my new coach. "We try to talk and she explodes in a tearful angry rage and stomps out of the room. Everything I say is taken out of context and used against me. I can barely open my mouth without her cutting me off and then leaving in a cloud of heated emotion."

My new coach redirected my focus off of my daughter and back onto myself. "I want you to think about the times in your relationship with your daughter when you have broken a promise or failed to keep an important commitment."

The suggestion caught me completely off guard. I was looking for tips on how to deal with an obstinate, irrational teenage girl, and I couldn't believe the relationship coach wanted me to think about promises I had made and broken. *Perhaps I hired the wrong coach*, I thought. But I persisted for another hour as she gave me several examples of people she had worked with who had restored trust through restoring integrity in their broken relationships.

"Have you ever considered," she asked in our second session, "that a lack of integrity may be the underlying cause of your challenges with your daughter?" That certainly was something I had never considered. I could relate with a lack of understanding or patience but a lack of integrity had never crossed my mind. And as I admitted to my coach,

I didn't really understand what integrity had to do with my present difficulties.

"Believe me," she said, "your integrity has everything to do with your challenges." She then gave me an assignment. "This weekend when you have some time alone, I want you to think back over the years with your daughter. Try to find a promise you made to her that you didn't keep or some agreement or commitment that you failed to honor. It may not be obvious at first, but I'd like you to give this some serious thought before we talk again on Monday."

That weekend was one I'll never forget. By nine o'clock on Sunday evening, I had discovered nothing. I could find no broken promises, no violated expectations or agreements not kept. That night my wife and I were looking through old family photo albums. There she was, on every other page, my little girl. The same one that seemed to dislike everything about me now, once so sweet and cute and kind. *What happened to that girl?* I wondered to myself.

My wife turned the page and I looked at a picture of our first apartment before we had any children. We began to reminisce about those days, so simple and relatively carefree. We were too poor to eat out or go to the movies, so we often walked around the beautiful neighborhoods behind our apartment complex. On many occasions our conversation turned to our future family. Both of us had come from strong, close families, and we talked about the kind of parents we had been blessed with and the kind of parents we wanted to be for our kids. Two things stood out above all others. We wanted a home where our kids felt loved unconditionally, where our family culture was so open and trusting that our kids could come to us and talk about anything—any problems or concerns, boyfriend and girlfriend difficulties, anything. We also wanted our home to be a safe place in every way. A place where, when our children were home, they felt completely comfortable: physically, emotionally, and spiritually. In these early days before kids came along, I had a crystal clear idea about the kind of father I wanted to be, and my wife was equally clear about her role as a mother.

Somewhere in that moment of recollection, the light dawned for me. As I reflected on my early conversations with my wife about the kind of parents we wanted to be one day and then thought about the war my daughter and I were engaged in, the mismatch was glaring. So was the broken promise, made years ago and playing out now, every time my daughter and I tried to talk. The promise I had made to myself, my wife, and our unborn children years earlier had been broken. I was not a kind, loving father that my daughter could talk to about anything—far from it. She could talk to me about nothing but silly, superficial topics that neither of us cared about. And as I blamed her for not listening and she blamed me for not understanding, our love began to diminish. That night I began, at least in part, to see why.

My conversation with my coach the next day was completely different from my previous head-scratching experiences. I told her of my ah-ha realization the night before, and she was ecstatic.

"Randy, this is the golden key, the great secret for you and your daughter. I know you can't see why right now, but I promise you, this is the mother lode." Over the next few days, she helped me map out how to restore integrity to my relationship with my daughter. The more we talked, the more I could see why keeping my word was so crucial in all my relationships and in every aspect of life. I had friends and colleagues who I really liked but who could never be relied on. Their promises were hollow and meant nothing. They weren't trustworthy. They had noble intentions and seemed sincere when they promised to do this or that, but at the end of the day, they rarely followed through. I saw how this affected their work, their ability to move up in the company, and even their family relationships. Everything in their lives was affected by their lack of integrity. And now, for the first time, I was beginning to see how I had unwittingly contributed to this important but wounded relationship.

But the more I anticipated talking with my daughter, the more anxious I grew. "You need to remember," I said to my coach, "when Jamie and I talk, it usually isn't pretty. It feels forced, probably for both of us. We're more like a couple of roommates who don't really like each other but who have to talk because they share the same dorm room and refrigerator."

"This conversation will be very different from any you have had before with Jamie," she reassured me. "This time you're going to clear up an old problem. Before, your conversations were only creating a bigger one." This was where I needed some hand holding. I realized as I thought about talking to Jamie that I didn't really know how to talk with her anymore—not without sparks flying. I felt helpless to direct the conversation down a positive and productive path, so we discussed a process for restoring integrity that can be applied to anyone in any area of life.

As luck would have it, our family had arranged a short vacation to a beautiful mountain retreat for the weekend. A bit anxious, I approached Jamie the first night we were there and asked if we could talk.

"What about?" she asked, clearly suspicious.

"Not about you or anything you've done. This time it's all about me and some stupid things I have done." This kind of conversation appealed to her sense of curiosity, as it would most teenagers. The next morning as the sun was rising over the lake, we sat outside with a stunningly beautiful backdrop.

Reluctantly, I began. "Honey, I have been thinking a great deal recently about our relationship, and I have some things I want to apologize for." Her eyes brightened with this prospect. "Now, before I say anything, let me reassure you that this has little to do with you or anything you have ever said or done. I'm blaming you for nothing. This is all about me and some things I realize I have failed to do, for which I am very sorry." I saw her immediately relax. After so many negative discussions in the past months, I could understand why she would fear that this was headed in a similar direction. Removing this fear was critical to creating an atmosphere where we could talk openly and honestly.

I shared some of my recent conversations with my coach and what I had learned. "I want to apologize for what I have said and done over the past few months that have created tension between us. All this time I thought this was all your fault. I've blamed you for our struggles and believed I had nothing to do with how things were going. Now I realize the truth, or at least some of it."

She sat patiently as I bumbled along, trying to recall what my coach had suggested. "I now see that I owe you a big apology. I have broken a promise I made to myself many years ago that you don't even know about."

"What promise, Dad?" she asked, genuinely intrigued at this point.

"Before you were ever born, Mom and I talked often about the kind of parents we wanted to be. I wanted to be the kind father that my children could talk to about anything. I wanted an atmosphere in our home where you could discuss any topic at any time and feel safe. We didn't want our children running to friends with their concerns and worries—we wanted you to come to us. And we knew that in order to have that kind of openness, we needed to love and listen in specific ways that made it easy for you to share with us whatever was on your mind."

"So what was the promise that you didn't keep?" she asked.

"Well, I wanted to be the kind of father that you could come to and talk about anything with, especially the hard, important things. While I didn't write it on a poster or carve it in stone, I certainly wrote it in my heart. I knew the kind of dad I wanted to be for my children, and I made a commitment to myself. I have failed to keep that promise, Jamie. You don't have the kind of father you can talk to. I'm not a father you feel listens to you without judging you or blaming you. Quite the opposite, the sad truth is that you can't talk to me about anything anymore. You're afraid to open up for fear of how I'll react—what I'll say or if I'll judge or blame you. I can clearly see that by failing to keep this promise I made years ago, it has greatly affected you and our relationship, and for that I'm truly sorry."

Jamie sat quietly, most likely overcome with shock. I wasn't criticizing nor blaming her. I had no interest in making her feel like the cause of our challenges. Instead, my former shabby behavior was simply a backlash for the earlier lapse in my integrity.

"I can also see that my actions have impacted me in many ways," I continued. "I don't have a relationship with you anymore, and that's not your fault, it's mine. I worry about you mostly because I have judged you as hard headed and angry, never thinking that your actions might be a reaction to my mistreatment, my blame and judgment of you. I've missed you, honey, and missed what we used to have. It saddens me to realize that all this time while I was blaming you, I've been missing the point, failing to see the truth of this situation. We've lost something very precious to me, and I want us to get it back, if we can."

She continued to sit quietly with her head lowered, perhaps in complete amazement. She was probably thinking, "What happened to this guy? Where did the old grouch go?"

"At this stage," I pressed on, "the only thing I can do is offer my sincere apology and ask for your forgiveness. I understand if you find it hard to forgive me, and I can't force you to do that. I realized before we sat down that whether you could forgive me or not, I still had to do what I had to do. I made a promise I failed to keep, and we have both experienced the painful consequences of my failure to honor my word."

She looked up with a smile and said, "Dad, you must not know me very well. Once someone sincerely apologizes as you have done, to me it's over. It's like it never happened. Of course I forgive you."

With the path now cleared, we could create a very different future for ourselves as father and daughter. I told her how I wanted things to be and realized that I had to make several changes. She wanted the same. We also discussed what would happen if I ever broke my promise in the future. She agreed to coach me and give me feedback when I drifted into the old patterns that had gotten us into the mess we had just cleaned up. At length we felt we had talked things through to the end. I hugged her and thanked her for listening and understanding. While it may sound like a Disney ending, I can honestly say that since that day, our relationship has never been the same.

While Jamie and I were talking, my wife came outside and saw that we were involved in a deep conversation. After Jamie went back in the cabin, my wife asked, "What was that all about? It looked pretty intense."

"Yes, it was intense, honey," I said. "But not for the reasons you might think. I believe I have just witnessed a transformation. Thirty minutes ago Jamie and I were entangled in a nasty pattern that was breaking our hearts. All of that has been healed with a simple, truthful conversation. It's like a miracle has taken place."

Since that unforgettable experience, I have not been the same. I cannot look on any relationship in my life as I once did. I see people all around me entangled in stressful relationships that they greatly dislike but feel they cannot change. When I ask them about their challenges, they serve up a healthy dose of reasons, explanations, theories, and excuses for why things with another person are eternally stuck in place, with little hope that things will ever improve. Like me, they feel they have done everything conceivable and that their relationship has continued to deteriorate. They have spent countless hours talking with others about how to mend this broken relationship. But their focus is always on the other person, on how to approach them differently, what to say and so forth. They think of everything save the one thing that cannot be overlooked.

The power of keeping our word at all times and with all people cannot be overstated. When I make a promise to you and keep it, integrity governs our interactions, and they are satisfying and easy. But when I fail to keep my word and turn to various excuses and reasons, our interaction is strained, trust is lost, and a productive relationship cannot be maintained. Your integrity with others determines, to a large degree, the quality of your relationships. Once it's lost, you lose something priceless. Even so, it is not impossible to reclaim what has been lost, as my experience with Jamie illustrates. Just as integrity can be lost, it can be restored. Though at times we break our word and fail to honor our commitments, we can apologize and restore our word to its rightful place. As my coach described it, integrity is the golden key, the magic secret that all of us look for but think we'll only discover when the other person changes. Others do change, to be sure, but that happens once we have reclaimed our own honor and restored trust in our relationships.

Not long ago I was teaching Sunday School, and an old friend began to complain about his son with whom a protracted cold war had set in. "He's lazy, refuses to go to school, won't listen to anyone who's honestly trying to help him, and basically sits around doing nothing and wasting his life."

"And I suppose you've told him all this a number of times?" I asked.

"Are you kidding? I've talked until I'm blue in the face, and it doesn't faze him. That kid is a lost soul, and I've basically given up on him."

"I wonder what it feels like when you know your dad has given up on you?" I responded. "Have you ever thought about that, John?" He didn't like my question.

"I can see that you are missing the point—just like he is," he snarled.

"When you're ready to heal this stormy relationship," I said, "I'd be happy to share with you what I've discovered. It's both easier and harder than you think." On that note, he turned and walked away, uninterested in what I had to say.

Why did this father walk away after my generous offer? Why wasn't he ready to make peace with his son? Because part of us enjoys being right more than being happy. To look honestly at yourself requires a degree of courage and humility that some people simply do not now possess. Integrity has a similar role as gravity. It reflects a natural law that all the talk in the world will never change. This embittered man will learn as we all do that if we want things to change for the better, we must change first. Stop blaming and judging. Stop excusing yourself for your mistreatment and lack of integrity because until you do, nothing will improve.

Making sense of our mortal challenges requires greater insight about the power of our word and the central role that integrity plays in every aspect of life. When our word becomes our bond, the possibilities for creating the kind of lives we want are limitless. Conversely failing to honor our word and having a weak relationship to our promises generates a host of problems within us and between us and others. Restoring integrity by honoring our word is absolutely essential. Lack of integrity is the underlying cause of so many of our stressful emotions. When we finally see and embrace this radiant truth, we're fully free to create different possibilities for ourselves and others.

THE PROCESS

When I share the story of my conversation with Jamie, many of my listeners want further detail on the steps I took, what I said first, second, and so on. I spent several hours thinking and planning for this conversation and created a simple but very useful road map for restoring my integrity. I'll share it here.

1. Identify the two or three areas in your life where you feel stuck and frustrated. This can include health, finances, or relationships—like with me and my daughter.

2. Now find the broken promises behind your frustrations. Rarely are these formal, written agreements but more often promises you made to yourself and to others, directly or not. You may have promised to get in shape, lose twenty pounds, or mend a broken relationship as I did. Now you know two things: the promises you made and the fact that you have failed to keep those promises. This is the root cause of some, if not all, of your negative emotion.

3. For promises you make to yourself, you simply need to restore integrity where it has been lost. This is easier than it sounds. You simply must make a promise and keep it. Do what you said you would do when you said you would do it. Herein lies your power

to create the kind of life you deeply desire. Restoring integrity is also a huge self-esteem booster as you gain mastery over your reasons, excuses, and rationalizing stories. Lack of integrity leaves you with the emotional fallout of failing to honor your word. You will discover a rich power source you never knew you had.

4. If you are restoring integrity to a relationship, here's the process I found very useful.

+   Begin by assuring the other person that this is not about him or anything he has done. It's about you and what you have done to bring tension and conflict into this relationship. This makes it easier for the other person to listen openly without feeling defensive or needing to protect himself from what you might say, given your history together.

+   Acknowledge where you failed to honor your word by describing the broken promise or violated agreement. Apologize for your lack of integrity.

+   Share the likely impact on him of what you have done. Ask if there are other ways your actions have impacted him. Then share the impact your failure has had on you. You might say something like, "I've made myself angry, blamed and resented you, and stewed over this for a long time. I see now that I brought all of this on myself by failing to keep my promise to you and others." Share any and all ways your own actions have impacted yourself and those around you.

+   Share what you'd like to see from this point forward. What kind of relationship would you like to have? What promises are you willing to make and keep to help bring this about? Share what you see as your ideal future relationship and assure the other person that he can count on you to keep your end of the new agreement. Gain his agreement to work on this new pattern together and to help one another stay on track.

+   Thank him for listening, for forgiving you, or at least for beginning to work toward forgiveness in the future. Apologize again, if necessary, for all you have done to create the pain and separation between you.

+   Most important, after all of this, keep your promises! If you fear that your word cannot be relied on, don't have this conversation.

Things will be far worse if you lay all of this out, clearly, sincerely, and honestly and then fail to keep your word again. Only you can make and keep your own promises. Don't undertake this kind of transformational process until you are ready to honor your word above all else.

The Dance of Doom

We begin with a curious riddle. How is it that otherwise successful, intelligent, and decent individuals become entangled in negative interactions that they do not like but cannot change? We're not talking about minor differences of opinion, personal preferences, or differences of interpretation. We are talking about the painful, stressful, wrenching interactions at home or work that serve as the source for our greatest stress and worry in life. Everywhere you turn, good relationships have gone bad, leaving those involved hurt, bitter, and angry.

Perhaps no set of stressful feelings are as taxing and trying as those that arise from our interpersonal challenges. These are disturbing for two reasons. First, we're never sure how it all started, although we can often think of something someone else said or did to ignite the feud. But worse, once entangled in negative interactions, we can't easily extract ourselves from them. In fact our best efforts to make things better often backfire, leaving us even more confused. We meet and talk, write letters, and explain the problem to countless others. But in the end, the dispute remains, creating a host of stressful feelings for all involved. In this chapter we're interested in two questions: How do we become entangled? And then, why can we not escape? With all our brains and experience, why can't we crack the code and resolve our people problems?

In my work with large corporations I have met brilliant business people, talented engineers, and computer scientists, all top-notch professionals who turn to mush when confronted with a broken relationship, especially at home. Many times over the years, I have sat at dinner with high-paid executives of Fortune 500 companies when the conversation turns to home and family.

These competent people turn to me and say something like, "I find the work you are doing with my company invaluable. But I'm wondering, how does this apply outside of work, say at home?" When I probe further, I learn about a bad marriage growing worse by the minute or a strained and negative interaction with a teenage son or daughter. My clients can make multi-million dollar decisions at work, speak three languages, and lead thousands of people into fierce competition with great success. But these same people are literally brought to their knees by a defiant teenage son or a spouse whose love has grown cold. When I ask them to tell me more about their relationship troubles, they usually report that they have tried everything to fix the situation and nothing has worked. Indeed many say that despite their best efforts at making things better, the distressing situation has actually gotten worse.

What could be more disconcerting? A key relationship in your life is no longer working and everyone knows it. Stress and worry are deepening, and feelings grow more intense. Both parties are confused and angry. Neither likes what is happening, but no one has any idea how to change the situation. The only logical solution you can think of requires the other person to stop what he is doing. While we may not openly try to get others to change, it's clearly what we're hoping will happen. And if that's not wrenching enough, we find, much to our dismay, that our best efforts to improve the situation backfire and things grow steadily worse. It can feel much like a frustrating chess match where every move you make gets you deeper and deeper into trouble from which you cannot escape. Knowledgeable chess players who play each move with a clear understanding of three or four moves ahead don't allow themselves to get trapped in no-win dead ends. We need this same kind of insight into our relationships with others.

UNDERSTANDING INTERACTION PATTERNS

There is an obvious difference between a casual acquaintance you see at the grocery store and a serious relationship at work or home. A *relationship* is characterized by two or more people interacting on a regular basis. The quality of the interactions, positive or negative, is cocreated. If I'm embroiled in a stressful relationship with my wife, we are creating our difficulties *together*. Focusing on the actions of one or the other partner fails to acknowledge that crucial interaction pattern created by the actions of both. Sometimes this is easy to see. The wife nags because her lazy husband refuses to get off the couch and help out around the house. She thinks if she doesn't nag him, nothing will ever get done. He refuses to help because she's always nagging him, to which she says, "If you would get up and help, I would stop nagging." Then he responds angrily, "Well, if you would leave me alone and stop nagging, maybe I'd do something." These pathetic patterns can roll on for years, becoming so entrenched that neither sees the part they play in first establishing and then perpetuating a pattern both dislike. What they can't see keeps them locked in the pattern. Blind to their role in the frustrating pattern, each persists at doing what they've always done, and growing more and more upset when things fail to change. They are unable to see that each *needs* the other to keep the pattern alive. He needs her nagging to justify his laziness, and she needs his laziness to justify her constant nagging—two people caught in a pattern they cannot surrender but can never win.

Even this silly pattern makes us scratch our heads. Why, for instance, doesn't the guy just get off the couch and do what his wife wants so she'll stop nagging him? Or why doesn't she stop hammering him to do what she wants if she knows he hates it? Why do we persist in doing the very thing that keeps the stressful interaction pattern alive, often for years? What keeps us stuck in something we both dislike? These are all useful and important questions we must understand if we ever hope to avoid the stress and strain of interpersonal conflict.

It's useful to think of relationships as a dance between you and others with whom you interact. Watch world-class ballroom dancers and you see this perfect rhythm as the movements of one are smoothly interwoven with the movements of the other. Imagine what would happen if in the middle of the tango, one of the dancers decided to fox trot. Chaos, confusion, and surprise would immediately set in. Each dancer relies in many ways on the actions of his partner in order to perform as well as he does. Neither can dance alone and neither can have a satisfying experience without the cooperation of the other.

Similarly a relationship is defined by the quality of the interaction between the individuals involved. In a marriage, the relationship is cocreated by the actions of one partner affecting and causing the reaction of the other. In a dance, both dancers could be world-class performers on their own, but once they become a partnership, there is a unique mixing of individual talents that is different from the skills of the two individuals involved. Applying this idea to a marriage, if you knew everything there was to know about each spouse—their personalities, preferences, habits, and hobbies—that still wouldn't tell you anything about the quality of their interaction. They might each be very nice as individuals, but together they cocreate a pattern that can be positive or negative. The way each behaves in relation to the other person defines the quality of their interaction. The behavior of one can only be understood in the context of the behavior of the other. Why a wife nags can only be understood by observing her husband's behavior and vice versa. If all we hear is the frustrating story of one or the other, we fail to see the full picture. When we do see the whole pattern, their individual complaints are much easier to understand.

Not long ago I received a call from a frustrated man who said his marriage was going down the tubes. I asked him to tell me the story, and he gave me the details of a good marriage gone bad after nearly twenty years. But despite all he told me of his side of the story and how his wife's actions affected him, I could not make sense of the marriage challenges in the context of their interaction. I had no idea what he was doing or failing to do, how she was affected, or how they responded to one another. Any focus on the individuals misses the crucial interaction dynamic that relationships create, for good or ill. All I knew was that the husband was saddened by his wife's strange behavior. But I didn't know why she was acting differently, and to ask him would only have given me more of the same story from his side. To make sense of any interaction challenge, you must view all parties in relation to each other. It is the interaction between individuals that reveals the pattern those individuals have unwittingly created.

A dance between two people in a marriage or work colleagues can be good or bad. I call negative, stressful interaction patterns a "dance of doom." This name aptly characterizes the doom loop that each individual in a relationship feels caught in when things become testy. When possible, and we see it every day, people simply give up trying to fix a broken relationship. In marriage they divorce. At work people are fired or they quit, completely convinced that no matter what they do, things will never improve. The problem is, if very little came from this experience and learning did not occur, similar patterns will be created in the next job or with the second wife or with the next employee. If we're helping to create negative interaction patterns but are blind to the part we play, we will continue to create similar outcomes and suffer the negative consequences they always bring.

I recently ran into a good friend who told me he was under a lot of stress at work. When I asked what was going on, he described a classic dance of doom. He was entangled in a rancorous relationship at work with a man who had once been a close friend, both in and outside of work. Their friendship had grown so bad that they passed one another in the hallways at work without even saying a word.

According to Dan, the breakdown began when he was passed over at work for a promotion he felt he deserved. The man who passed him over was his former friend. Dan felt snubbed, took it personally, and resented his colleague for not giving him what he deserved. That day, Dan made a decision with far-reaching consequences. He blamed and resented his former friend and refused to have any more to do with him—a bit tricky given that their offices were across the hall from one another. Dan seethed as they sat in meetings and business decisions were made that would directly affect him, while his former friend seemed completely indifferent to Dan's plans and concerns.

By the time Dan sat in my office and detailed his entire sad scenario, he was ready to quit and walk away. "I don't think I can handle it anymore," he said wearily. "I can barely drag myself into work anymore. I'm totally stressed out over this entire experience."

When dancing the dance of doom with another person, we are stricken with mental blindness, but of course we don't realize it. Dan would have said that the reason he was stressed out was because of how people like his former friend had mistreated him. He would have ticked off the various wrongs done to him by others in the company, never once mentioning anything he had done to deserve such mistreatment. In fact this is one of the standard features of those caught up in the dance of doom. They feel totally innocent of any wrongdoing. Thus the other person is not only unkind but grossly unfair. It is the other person who is judging and blaming them for things they did not do. While

Dan could confess all the many sins of his former friend and provide a detailed blow-by-blow of the wrongs committed against him, he portrayed himself as a perfect angel who had done nothing wrong, certainly nothing bad enough to deserve this kind of treatment. Dan felt blamed and judged harshly by his former friend, which made him defensive. But when we feel others are attacking us, as Dan did, we think we have no other choice but to defend ourselves. It's what we can't see at such times that keeps the fires of conflict raging.

Anyone who has ever become entangled with another person knows how emotionally draining it can be. It consumes us with a complex mix of emotions from fear and hurt to anger and deep frustration. What's more, we think that our burdensome emotions are caused by those with whom we dance. We are convinced that others are "making" us feel as we do and that if they would change, our stress would go away. We may admit that we're hurt and angry, even stressed out, but still we blame the other party, who we believe makes us feel as we do. Then we not only resent them for what they are doing but for the kind of person they force us to be.

I asked Dan what attempts he had made to resolve his conflict at work. His answer was typical of someone caught in a painful interaction.

"I've done everything I can do. Now it's his turn to do something."

"So, what exactly have you done?" I asked further. "Have you talked with him about your feelings, shared your concerns, tried to work through your differences in a productive way? What do you feel you have done to mend this relationship?"

He said nothing for several moments. My question caught him off-guard. "No, I haven't done any of that," he finally admitted. "But there's no more I can do at this stage. If he would sit down and apologize to me, then maybe we could pull things together. But until that happens, there's little for me to do except quit. He'll never apologize. We don't even talk anymore."

This is also a typical reaction. Our strong negative emotion prevents us from doing the only productive thing we can do. When I asked Dan if he had sat down and talked to his friend about all of this, he looked at me as if to say, "Do you think I'm crazy? I'm not talking to that guy." What he could not see—but that was so clear to me—was how his bitterness and unwillingness to openly talk with his friend helped sustain their negative interaction. While Dan could easily tell me what he hated about work and his old friend, he could not even guess why his friend was reacting so coolly to him. "He has hurt and injured me," Dan said. "I have done nothing to him. So what have I got to say to him, even if we did talk?"

The mental blindness caused by the dance of doom makes a simple situation feel very complicated. Myopic and innocent, we can see nothing but the unacceptable actions of another and are completely blind to anything we have done. Thus we feel unjustly mistreated. Furthermore, our logic is distorted. While we resent and blame the other person for what he is doing to us, we feel we have done nothing to deserve his mistreatment. We use *emotional logic* that makes sense within our confused and turbulent mind but makes no sense to outsiders. To me it seemed a simple thing for Dan to go to work the next day and sit down, talk over his differences with his coworker, and see if they could mend old fences. But the determination to be right and make others wrong runs deep when we are caught up in a painful pattern with others that we feel we did not start nor help to sustain. We feel innocent and victimized while to us the other person is clearly guilty and wrong.

Dan had come to my office looking for advice, coaching, and input on how to handle this difficult situation. Usually in such situations, people are looking for better ways to handle the difficult people with whom they must work. Essentially they say, "I have a very difficult and stressful relationship at work that I cannot understand. How do you suggest I cope with the difficult people in my life?" Dan was about to learn that the key to his peace had nothing to do with his friend or how he had been mistreated. The last place he would think to look for legitimate solutions would be the first place he must examine.

"I think I have a pretty good idea of what you're wrestling with at work," I said. "But let me ask you another question. Do you really want to end this painful situation or not? How important is this to you, Dan?"

"I've reached the point where I can't continue to drag myself into work another day unless things change." When we say things like this what we mean is, "How do I get this person to treat me differently? How can I get him to stop doing what he's doing that's causing me so much stress?" We are not thinking about what we could do to resolve our differences. Our twisted logic has us thinking that we have done nothing wrong, so therefore, we have nothing to change. If we had caused the problems, then we could fix them, but as innocent victims of another person's mistreatment, we feel helpless. It's this thought that lies at the center of our internal tension and stress.

"I think I understand what your friend has done that causes you so much angst and stress," I said to Dan. "Put another way, I understand the kind of person you must respond to. Let's look at the other side for minute. What kind of person are you being for him? You can easily see that you are simply reacting to his mistreatment of you. If he treated you with more respect and valued your contribution, you would treat him differently, right?"

"Yes," said Dan quickly. "If he would make the first move, then I would treat him differently. But I shouldn't have to be the one to go to him and resolve our differences when he caused all of this."

"Well, let's look at both sides of your issue. Think of yourself and the other guy—your old friend. What kind of person is he being for you? It's that person who you resent and blame for what has happened. You feel as you do because of what this other person has said and done, right?" Dan nodded in agreement. This side of the dance of doom makes sense to us. "But at the same time, Dan, your friend also has another person with whom he must find a way to interact more effectively. You are that other person for him, just as he is the other person for you. Each of you is reacting to what the other man is doing. So just like you think he is causing your pain, he likely feels the same way about you. The critical question for you to think about is this: What kind of person are you being for him? What sort of other man are you for him?"

At this point our mental blindness can be deadly. Dan had never considered any question along these lines. He was obsessed and intently focused on blaming his friend for the situation. As a result he had no room in his "viewfinder" for himself. With such a narrow point of view, we cannot see ourselves in relation to them. We can only see what they are doing to us, and we know all too well how it makes us feel. This leaves us totally out of touch with how we are impacting others, which is why we go on mistreating them as we do. We may feel they deserve it for all the wrongs they have committed, but there's something we cannot see that we must understand. When I see the kind of person I am being for those with whom I dance, I begin to see a more complete picture of the dance in which I am entangled. I not only see how they step on my toes, but I begin to see how I kick them in the shins. I begin to see that what I do matters, for I react to you just as you react to me.

Most people caught in the dance of doom can only see a narrow viewpoint of their troublesome situation. This blindness leads to hard hearts and lack of compassion for what others face as they react to us each day.

The only way to end a stressful pattern with another person is to ask these kind of questions. What Dan had been doing was clearly not working, but his determination to be right and innocent, and his subsequent need to blame others, pressed him down a dead-end path, irrespective of the costs. Turning the focus from others to ourselves is essential. If we are simply responding to them, then *they* are responding to *us*. So if we can more clearly see the kind of people we are being, we can shift the way we're dancing and change the style of our interaction. This demands honest, sincere self-observation, which is hard to come by when our hearts have grown hard.

In her book *The Dance of Anger*, Harriet Lerner explains, "Self observation is the process of seeing the interaction of ourselves and others, and recognizing that the ways other people behave with us, has something to do with the ways we behave with them. We cannot make another person be different, but when we do something different ourselves, the old dance can no longer continue as usual."[1]

Dan was still thinking about my questions. I wanted him to shift the focus from his friend to himself. He knew what kind of person his former friend was presenting to him. It was the person Dan was required to react to day after day. But I had asked Dan to reflect on the kind of person *he* was being.

Having been in his shoes, I knew this was something he had never considered. Our strong negative emotions cloud our rational thinking, which is why we behave so irrationally. To onlookers we continue doing the very things that keep us embroiled in a stressful interaction. But we can't see it, and from our myopic point of view we are doing the only thing we can do given the circumstances. We even think things like, *I would treat them differently if they would treat me differently*. Like immature children who hit one another because "he hit me first," we engage in a silly but painful "tit for tat" pattern. We'll be nice if they'll apologize and treat us nicely first. But of course those with whom we dance are thinking the same thing. This is how we become locked in negative patterns that we greatly dislike but can't seem to change. We blame them and wait for them to change, apologize, and make things right. Meanwhile, they are doing the same thing for very similar reasons.

Giving others a different person to respond to automatically changes the nature of the interaction pattern. Even the slightest move different from our standard response requires the other person to respond differently. For instance, if I resent you for not talking to me, and one day you say hello and spend a few minutes chatting, I cannot respond as I did before because I'm not responding to that person. I'm now responding to someone who talks to me, and that requires me to change. My former indifference matched up with your indifference to me, tit for tat. But when you change, ever so slightly, you give me a different person to respond to. As such, my old reaction no longer matches what I am receiving from you.

"Right now, Dan," I continued, "Your old friend is responding to you as an angry, embittered former friend who refuses to talk to him. You pass by him in the hall and accuse and resent him for all your troubles at work. That's who you are being for him right now, true?" It was true and Dan knew it. "So, given the kind of person you are being, are his actions all that surprising?" He shook his head with understanding. "And here's what's interesting," I persisted. "You claim that the only reason you are treating him this way is because of how he treats you. You justify your mistreatment of him by pointing your judgmental finger at everything he is doing that is wrong. But the real question, Dan, is this. What are you doing that's wrong? What about the blame and resentment you have heaped on him? What about the backbiting at work and home when he's not around? You might blame him for some things, but you clearly can't hold him responsible for what you're doing. That's all you. I don't say that to blame you in any way, just to help you see the kind of person you are presenting to him, which provokes exactly what you are seeing. If you really want him to treat you differently, then you must give him a different Dan to respond to. Let the old, bitter, angry Dan leave. Replace him with one who goes to your friend; apologizes for what he has said, felt, and thought; and seek to put the pieces back together again."

Dan sat quietly through all of this and finally gave a heavy sigh and said, "I'm not sure I can do that, Randy."

"Let me ask you this," I continued. "How would you like your friend to respond to you differently from how he does now? Ideally, how would you like him to treat you, respond to you, think about you, and so on?"

"I want him to respect me and give me credit for what I do and how I contribute to the company's success," answered Dan matter-of-factly. "I want him to acknowledge me rather than acting like I don't even exist."

"That makes sense. If I were you, I would want those kinds of things as well. So here's the question. If that's how you would like him to respond to you, what can you do to encourage his respect? What kind of person would you need to be in order for him to respect you more and acknowledge your work?"

He stared out the window for a moment and then said, "I'm not sure."

"Let's turn it around and see how it might look from your point of view. If your friend wanted more of your respect and appreciation, what might he do to encourage that from you? If he ignored you at work, refused to talk to you, and blamed you for his problems, would that do it?" Dan smiled at the absurdity of this suggestion.

"Of course not" he admitted. "I guess he would need to come to me, share with me what's happening at work, involve me in what he's doing so I'm in the loop. Then I can see what he's doing and acknowledge him for it."

"And what if he didn't? What if every time the two of you were in the same room, he ignored you, and you could feel the tension between you. What if you knew he blamed you resented you for his problems at work? What if you saw how friendly he was with others but not to you? Would that make you want to respect him more and increase your desire to reach out and acknowledge his efforts?"

"I don't think that would help," Dan admitted with a deep sigh.

"So can you see how this works? Can you begin to see that in a relationship, the actions of one have a direct impact on the actions of the other? You respond to his treatment of you, and he responds to your treatment of him. Just like two dancers who play off one another, one leads, the other follows, and as the other follows, the other continues to lead. It is what you create *together* that disturbs you both."

Dan said nothing, thinking about what I had said.

Two concerns distract us from positive change: a determination to be "right" and our efforts to make the other person wrong. We often tell a story of how the other person started it, much like two kids scuffling over a toy. "He started it" is the defense every kid has used for thousands of years to justify mistreating their playmates. Dan was stuck in this same mind-set. We think that if the other person started the dispute, then we are justified in our mistreating him thereafter. He cheated first so when I cheat I am only doing it because he forced me into it; therefore, it's not really cheating. He made me do it, and I resent him for it. This kind of thinking shifts the focus of the interaction pattern both are creating and places it on the individuals involved. By focusing exclusively on what his friend was doing and how he felt his friend had betrayed him, Dan lost all sight of his own involvement in his troubling situation.

At this point I felt I had one last chance to help Dan see what needed to happen in this painful relationship. "As I see it," I told Dan, "you have two options. One is to keep doing what you're doing. But you must ask yourself a question if you decide to remain stuck in this old pattern: What could you possibly gain by continuing to resent and blame your friend? You already know where that leads. Besides, if you honestly want him to respect and acknowledge you more than he now does, blaming, resenting, and avoiding him is a strange way to go about it, wouldn't you agree?"

He looked up at me and nodded. "But, Randy—"

"There are no 'buts' anymore, Dan," I interrupted. "When you think, 'I would change but . . .' you are resisting any responsibility for what has happened between you. Your current relationship has been created by both of you. He can't have a stressful relationship without you, and you can't have one without him. It requires the cooperation and the collusion of both to create such a negative and painful interaction pattern. When you present him with a different person than the one you have been for so long, it evokes a change from him. Isn't this what you really want, anyway? Don't you want him to treat you differently and show you more respect? You just told me that was what you really wanted. To have him respond differently to you, you must be a different person for him. If you remain as you are, so will he. Your change gives him a reason to change as well. That's how interaction patterns work, Dan—whether you believe it or not."

He had no response to my comments. But, as he put on his coat to leave, he said, as a parting shot, "I know I should probably talk with this guy and clear the air, but I'm not sure I want to give him the satisfaction."

Blame is an integral part of the dance of doom. The logic is simple. Whoever is to blame is the one who's responsible. When we think we are an innocent victim of another's mistreatment, we are consumed with blame and resentment for what he is doing. We feel mistreated for no logical or legitimate reason. With all the blame and responsibility placed entirely on the other person, we feel we have nothing to say to him, nothing to do but wait for him to come around. And so we wait, seething with anger, hurt, and stressed while the other person copes as best he can with someone who resents him. This once again reflects a gross misunderstanding about how relationships work. We cannot focus on the individual actions of one or the other. That isn't helpful. That leads to questions such as, "Who started it? What did he say or do and why?" Does it really matter who started it when both are being affected? Does it really matter who fired the first shot if both sides are killing one another six months later?

This is what Dan was suggesting when he said he wasn't willing to give his opponent the satisfaction. If Dan went to the other man and talked things out, Dan's twisted logic assumed that would look like Dan shared in the blame for what had happened. That would look like Dan had a part in the fall out and he didn't think he did. You can almost see Dan pounding his fist on the desk and crying bitterly, "I am innocent. I have done nothing to deserve what has happened here. I refuse to take the blame for any of this."

But, of course, it's this arrogant reaction that prevents others from coming to him. Clearly to blame others for something that has affected two people fails to take into account all parties involved. It's like saying, "We have a problem and it's all your fault." Can you imagine two dancers talking to one another like this? If they do, they won't be partners very long. Good dancers realize that it's what they create *together* that matters and that they cannot dance alone. "You affect me, and I affect you," is the central truth that evades us as we devote so much emotional energy to being right and making others wrong.

If the patterns we've been discussing were not so deeply frustrating for those involved, they would almost be comical. While the specific details vary, the basic "tit for tat" pattern remains unchanged. Blame and resentment of others lies at the heart of all stressful interactions. Blind to the part we play in our people problems, we feel we have done nothing to deserve their mistreatment. As a result, we feel innocent and right and judge others as guilty and wrong. Our innocence, however, leaves us in a difficult spot. Confident that we have no part in the dispute, we feel we can have no part in the solution. Hence, the only thing we can do is hang around until the other person changes. But he won't change because of our judgment and blame. There is great irony in all of this. We want the other person to change and treat us with more respect. And what do we do to get him to change? We blame him and resent him for how we think he makes us feel. We blame him not only for what he does but also for the kind of person he turns us into. He makes us crazy, stresses us out, and causes our anger and deep frustration. So we lay all of this at the feet of those with whom we dance and are puzzled and frustrated when they fail to change.

The good news is that the process of creating a positive interaction pattern is exactly the same as the process of creating a negative one. Being unwilling to take any responsibility keeps us locked in painful patterns that we do not like but cannot seem to change. Since both parties are co-creating their interaction pattern, both are responsible. When we begin to see how what we do helps evoke the kind of mistreatment we see from others, then we can stop the insanity by changing how we dance with them. But if we're too attached to being right and making others wrong, a resolution will never work.

CHANGING THE DANCE

If you are caught up in a stressful relationship similar to those we've been discussing, it's time to end the dance of doom and dance a new dance: the dance of joy, peace, and genuine love and acceptance. Always remember—stressful, negative feelings never come from God. No matter what the circumstances might be, our situation cannot compel us to blame, judge, and resent others. That is simply not the Lord's way. It is, however, exactly how Satan can make us miserable and wretched. Disputation, discord, and contention always stir our hearts up unto anger, and once we're angry and feel we're not responsible, Satan has us right where he wants us (see 3 Nephi 11:29). The key is to end these painful patterns as quickly as possible, thereby minimizing the hurt we feel and the hurt we cause those with whom we're dancing. The good news is that ending these patterns is much easier than we suppose. It involves changing our point of view, changing our minds, and changing our hearts. If we're unwilling to change any of these, we had best settle in for a long, painful, and heartbreaking dance of doom—for it can end in no other way.

Here are several suggestions for breaking the burdensome and negative patterns that ensnare you:

1. On a piece of paper create two columns. In the left column, write down your thoughts about the situation. How you feel about the other person, what you resent most, what you dislike most, what you think your opponent should do that he is not doing. Capture as best you can the essence of your complaint against the other person.

2. In the right column, write down how you think the other person sees you. What does he say about you? What do you think he might be thinking about the way you interact with him? As best you can, view this situation from his point of view. This is not an attempt to ascertain who's right or wrong, who's more at fault, who started it, or any of that. That's where we typically want to focus and why we're entangled in the mess we're currently in.

3. If you look at both columns, you should see a clear connection. How you think, feel, and act is the kind of person your opponent is responding to and how he thinks, feels, and acts is the person you are responding to. Just like two people dancing, each of you is unwittingly thinking, saying, and doing the very things that keep the painful dance alive. Seeing this cause and effect relationship is essential, for in so doing, you begin to see the part you play in what afflicts you. Most of us know all too well what others do to hurt our feelings, make us angry, or offend us. But rarely can we see the part we play, the kind of person we are being to our opponent.

4. If you've done this exercise honestly, you should have some insight into the darkness of your previous confusion. Now you understand that you are helping create the problems you complain about and doing the very things that will ensure that it keeps rolling painfully along. This tells you what you must not do any longer if you want the dance of doom to end. Why? Because what you are now doing is what provokes the other person to mistreat you just as what he is doing provokes yours.

5. I've said many times, give your opponent a different person to respond to. Practically speaking, this often involves repenting of your blame and resentment. What another person does is actually not your business. Your business is what you think and say. For it is these toxic thoughts and emotions that make you miserable, not the actions of others. You must change how

you see and think about the other person, and you must take responsibility for all that you possibly can.

For example, in the story of Dan's rotten relationship with his former friend, he could go to his friend and say, "Jim, can we talk? I want to apologize for how I've been acting. I've walked by you in the hallway like you're a total stranger, and after all we've been through together, that's silly, immature, and ridiculous. For all of that, I'm sorry. I'm sure I've made it hard for you to come to work with me treating you so disrespectfully. I'd like to get back on track and try to repair the damage. I hope this will be a start."

Notice what's happening in this short, simple, but powerful conversation. First and foremost, Dan is giving his old friend a *different* Dan than he's seen in months. This change requires Jim to change as well. Formerly Jim was responding to a cold, distant, resentful old friend who wouldn't give him the time of day. Now Dan stands in Jim's office, sincerely apologetic and interested in rebuilding what they once had—no blame, no attempt to excuse his behavior, no superficial sales-pitch slogans to get Jim to come around. Dan disarms Jim from any defensiveness because there is nothing for Jim to defend against—no attacks, no blame, no accusations, no anger. None of it. Also, Dan retains his power to transform this stressful relationship by taking responsibility for the wrong things he has, in fact, thought, said, and done. Blame has absolutely no power. The power to create positive change begins when we take full responsibility for our part, acknowledge it to those who need to hear it, and propose a different kind of relationship in the future.

And how will Jim react to all of this? In all likelihood, his heart will be convicted by his own mistreatment of Dan. Jim could have made the first move but didn't and now that Dan has come to him, he opens to the door to real reconciliation. When I've been part of such transformations, I always feel like I've been witness to a miracle. Two people who have fallen into a painful pattern, deeply stressful to both, transcend their differences by one or the other changing. This invites the compassion and empathy from the other party. This is the Lord's way. Now, let us do it.

Notes

1. Harriet Lerner, *The Dance of Anger: A Woman's Guide to Changing the Patterns of Intimate Relationships* (New York: HarperCollins, 1997).

DISTURBING
YOURSELF

The following sentiment has been stated a thousand ways over the centuries but never better than when it was originally penned by the Greek philosopher Epictetus: "We are disturbed not by events, but by the views which we take of them."[1] Day by day as you and I face large and small difficulties, some stern indeed, something else accompanies our trying circumstances—*our thoughts about that experience.* Initially there is the event itself. A sobering diagnosis from a doctor, a critical exam failed, the end of a twenty-year marriage, a rebellious and troubled child, a lost job, weeks spent without finding another job, and so on. We could never capture the length and breadth of challenges, setbacks, and surprises that confront us in life. Such experiences trigger first an intellectual reaction as we immediately begin to think about the event, but it is the thinking that accompanies a difficult experience that causes our emotional pain. Thus we are not actually disturbed, stressed, or weighed down by the event itself but by the kinds of thoughts we generate about that event. It's not what happens to us that disturb us. In reality we disturb ourselves by the stressful thoughts we have about what has happened. This is a profound insight and a critical key to making sense of our trials, setbacks, and negative surprises.

For example, I met with a man recently who was greatly disturbed by the events in his life. Rob had met a woman whom he firmly believed was "the one," but after several months of dating and talks of marriage, she ended the relationship. Rob was crushed. Day after day he nursed his sorrows and dragged everyone he could into his pity party. He couldn't sleep, lost interest in nearly everything, and even let his troubles affect his performance at work. People began to avoid him so they wouldn't have to listen to his sad story of rejection and love lost, which he freely told to anyone who would listen and sympathize. When his distress spilled over into his work performance, he was told to get some professional help. Soon thereafter, Rob sat across from me in my office.

In his hands were copies of letters he had written to his former soul mate. He asked if he could read a few of them so I could better understand his situation. I agreed but soon realized I had agreed too soon. He launched into a detailed, blow-by-blow account of what she had done, what he had said, how she had responded, and what he had told her about what she had said. My head was spinning. A couple pages into his lengthy heart-wrenching treatise, I interrupted.

"I think I get the essence of what's going on," I said. "Let's spend the rest of our time trying to understand why you feel as you do and how to free yourself from your distress. Would that be okay?"

"Well, I just thought you would need to know the background of the situation. I actually have several more letters here if you think it would be helpful."

"No," I said quickly, "that won't be necessary, but thanks for offering." He would soon realize that I was far less interested in what had happened and why than I was in his current *thoughts* about the situation. Since it's not our difficult experiences that trouble us but the way we think about, interpret, and explain them to ourselves and others, that's where the real mother lode can be found. Think of the hours of therapy that could be done to wade through the lengthy and detailed history, reading through his ream of letters and journal entries about having met the perfect woman and then losing her to the arms of another man. His experience could serve as juicy fodder for reality TV, but dwelling on it would not help him move on. Rob was deeply disturbed by stressful thoughts that sorely afflicted him. His life had been turned upside down by this experience, but through it all he had drawn one very erroneous conclusion. As he sat in my office with his letters, heartache, and tears, he firmly believed that this tragic situation had caused him to feel as he did. It was the breakup that was doing this to him—the lost love, the possibility of how things might have been for him with the love of his life, now lost and gone forever. He believed that what had happened *to him* was the cause of his deep anguish. That was untrue. His turmoil and emotional pain flowed directly and automatically from his *thoughts* about the situation, not from any part of the situation itself.

This is far more than just a play on words. It represents a fundamental difference in how we explain and resolve the emotional pain that afflicts us when we encounter trials, setbacks, and surprises in life. When we think that circumstances are causing our pain, we are left powerless. After all, what could this man do that he hadn't already tried in order to change his circumstance? He had pled with her to come back and had written her scathing letters about her new boyfriend and what a terrible mistake she was making choosing that rascal over him. He had whined to friends, complained bitterly to work colleagues, prayed and cried, and prayed some more that somehow she would come back around. Nothing had changed. In fact, from what I could gather, his obsession over her had driven her further away, not reeled her in as he had so desperately hoped. Whenever we think that our stressful feelings are caused by our external circumstances, we have so few options. In reality we have two choices—either we can try to change the circumstance, or we can change how we think about the circumstance. In most cases, we try the first, since the circumstance appears to be the cause of our distress.

On the other hand, when we learn to see our circumstances differently, we retain our power to transcend our stressful feelings since they are nothing more than extensions of our thinking. This sad man was depressed because of his thoughts about his experience, not by the specific situation itself. Put another way, it was not his disappointing situation that disturbed him but how he thought about the situation. One he can do little about, the other he has absolute mastery over. Often it is difficult, if not impossible, to change what has happened to us, but we can always change our thinking about what has happened.

I directed his attention to the Epictetus quote framed on my office wall. "We are disturbed not by events, but by the views which we take of them."[2]

"What do you think this means, Rob?" I asked.

He paused to read it again and sat for a moment or two pondering on it. "I guess I'm not sure," he admitted. "Seems like if you are in a difficult situation, things can get pretty upsetting and stressful. I guess

I'm not sure what this guy is trying to say."

I've shared this quote with many people over the years, and Rob's answer was fairly typical. Most people can't see a difference between a difficult experience and their thinking about that experience. Why? Because our thinking occurs simultaneously with the experience, or at least it seems that way. One minute we feel at peace, positive, and upbeat. Suddenly the phone rings and we learn that a friend has been in an automobile accident. Thankfully it's not serious, but she'll be in the hospital for a few days. In a split second our feelings change from happy and positive to sad and worried. It appears that the news about our friend caused our sadness, which is partly true. But rarely are we aware of the thoughts that accompany such experiences and that foreshadow how we feel. Even the simple thought, "Oh, this is terrible" will produce negative feelings. But when we hear the accident wasn't serious, another thought replaces the first and our feelings shift. All of this occurs with such lightning speed that we scarcely notice it.

It's useful to think of experiences occurring in two stages. First an event occurs in which we have various thoughts that generate our feelings, positive or negative. The event or basic facts in any given situation carry no emotional charge. The phone rings, a voice on the other end tells you about the accident, and then you think (judge, explain, or interpret) what that event means to you. This is how I explained it to Rob.

"In any situation there are the basic facts and there are your thoughts or interpretation about those facts. Facts are neutral. They're just facts. Let's examine your situation. You were dating a woman you really liked. You thought she was the one for you, the woman of your dreams. Then, for various reasons you've shared, you stopped dating, and now she is dating someone else. Are these the basic facts in your story?"

"Pretty much," he said with a sigh.

"Okay, so let's return to the observation by Epictetus. You are not disturbed by these facts. By themselves, basic facts can't disturb you. They certainly don't disturb me at all. You were dating a woman and now you're not. You have lots of story before, during, and after this basic summary fact, but this is essentially the bottom line, right?" He nodded, with a curious look as to where I was headed with this sermon.

"So, Rob, why do you think your sad, depressing story doesn't make me sad and depressed? Why am I not disturbed by your experience the way you are?"

"Well, that's easy," he shot back with little hesitation. "It's not your problem. You didn't lose the perfect woman. This doesn't affect you like it does me. You don't care if I see her again or not, but I do. I'm not asking you to care, but I thought you would understand why this is so hard for me."

"It's not that I don't care. It's simply that I think differently about the facts than you do. Neither of us are affected by what's happened, only by our differing thoughts about it. For instance, share with me your primary thoughts that disturb you the most when you think about what has happened between you and this woman."

"I just can't get over it. I think of her constantly. I think of how it used to be and how perfect we were for each other. I'm always thinking about the plans we made and the vacations we talked about, the things we wanted to do after we got married. Now all of that is gone, and try as I may, I'm helpless to get her back. I don't know if I'll ever get over it, and that worries me as much as anything else." He buried his head in his hands and groaned. When engulfed by stressful feelings, it is hard to think clearly and see how we are unwittingly bringing upon us the pain that these feelings inflict.

"Now, Rob, I see how you feel," I said, treading carefully. "May I share with you my thoughts about your situation?"

"Sure," he said, lifting his head to look at me. "I can use whatever help you can offer."

"Remember, the only reason I don't feel exactly as you is because of how I think about what has happened to you. If I thought you had actually lost the only woman for you and if I believed that you could never be happy with anyone else, that thought would sadden me. But that's not what I think, and I'm suggesting that your freedom from these burdensome emotions that oppress you will come when you think differently about what has occurred."

"I don't know how to think differently, Randy. I've tried to put this out of my mind, and, like a ghost, it haunts me day and night. I've tried to forget her and move on, but I can't. I keep thinking that there's still something I could say or do to get her back, but she's moved on. She's already found a new boyfriend, and they parade right in front of me at church as if she and I were never a serious couple. I can hardly handle going to church anymore, knowing that she'll be there with him and will say nothing to me. That's what kills me the most."

"Let's talk about what you just said. You think you have lost the perfect woman for you, the woman of your dreams—is that correct?" Rob nodded. "Let me ask a couple questions: Is that really true? Can you know with 100 percent certainty that you have lost the woman of your dreams? Can you really know that this was the woman you were supposed to marry?"

"I have believed that from the first time I saw her."

"And I'm asking you to think about that. Can you really know that this one specific woman is the only woman for you? Can you really know that for sure?"

"Well, I suppose I can't know for sure, but I certainly wanted things to turn out that way."

"And that's the source of your pain, Rob," I continued. "You thought things would and should take one path and instead they took a different one. You thought the two of you would marry and live happily ever after, and now she is dating another man less than a month after breaking up with you. You simply want things to be different from how they really are, Rob. And whenever we resist and resent things as they really are, we bring upon ourselves a tide of stressful feelings. Does that make sense to you?"

"Kind of," he said pensively. "Because things have turned out different from how I thought they would turn out, it depresses me."

"Yes and the key word in what you just said is 'thought.' It isn't your breakup with her that hurts, but your thoughts about the breakup, the way you interpret that experience. That's what causes you so much emotional pain. You believe your life is over—that the only woman who could ever make you happy has chosen a different man. You fear that you will never find anyone close to her and all of that bundled together and ruminated on constantly is making you miserable. That is a sad and stressful story and because you believe it's true, you suffer."

I could see that I had finally gotten his attention. In the deep hole of despair into which his thoughts had cast him, he had lost all hope. A loss of hope always feeds on itself, making us increasingly more wretched. When we finally realize that it is only our thoughts that have cast us into the pit, hope is born anew.

"Are you making the connections, Rob? Do you see how your thoughts and stressful story about what has happened is the real cause of your deep sorrow and pain? Can you understand that as long as you continue to think as you now do, your pain will grow worse, not better? And this isn't really about you, Rob, but about your thoughts.

"You are not your thoughts and I am not mine. If I adopted your way of thinking about a similar situation in my life, I would feel very much as you now feel. Stressful thoughts always produce stressful, burdensome feelings. As the night follows the day, this is how it works for everyone. Can you see more clearly what this insightful quote has to do with you?"

"Yes, I think so," he said slowly. "I think I needed your help in thinking about it differently. I've been so consumed by this whole situation, I didn't know how to view it any other way."

"Great, let's do it right now," I said. "You told me you can't know that this really was the woman of your dreams. You thought she was, but you really can't know for certain. But when you believe she was the one for you and you lost her, that is a very stressful thought, generating a ton of dark, dreary feelings. So if your present thoughts cause these dark feelings, let's consider different thoughts, opinions, or interpretations of what has happened. You have said you lost the perfect woman. That makes you very sad. Turn that thought around and see how it feels."

"I didn't lose the perfect woman," he said, a bit puzzled.

"That's right—you didn't lose the perfect woman. And you know how I know that? Because the woman you thought was so perfect for you is dating another man. If she's perfect for you, why is she dating him? Besides, if she's so perfect for you and you two were so deeply in love, why did she pick up on another guy so quickly after you broke up? Is that the kind of woman you want to marry, one who has such a tenuous emotional tie to you that at the drop of a hat she's gone to someone else?"

"That's true," he said with a smile. "I hadn't really thought of that side of it."

"And when you think of that side of it, what do you notice? How do you react emotionally to the possibility that you did not lose the perfect woman but may have dodged a bullet? I'm not saying that's true. I'm just throwing out other possibilities to the one you came in here with. Your basic thought was 'I've lost the perfect woman and it's killing me.' I'm suggesting a different possibility. You didn't lose the perfect woman because if she was really 'the one,' you would both be together in love right now. But, instead, she is off with some other guy while you cry your eyes out and surrender to deep depression. So let's take the story of you losing the perfect woman off the table, and all we have left are the facts. You were dating this woman, you liked her, and she liked you, but she decided to stop dating you and start dating someone else. Remember, you have no story or interpretation of any of this. They are the basic facts and nothing more. Without your sad, heart-breaking story of love lost, what do you notice? How does it look to you?"

I could see a dawning in his eyes.

"Without my story this really shouldn't bother me at all. Without my story I feel sort of lucky that I found out now rather than later that she wasn't that committed to me. And without my story, I wouldn't be so consumed with darkness, despair, and pain."

"That makes sense to me" I replied. "Our strong negative emotions are powerful and useful signals to tell us that there's something askew in our thinking. That's what I hear you saying. You thought you had lost the perfect woman, and now you realize that's not true. Take away all the drama, all the shattered dreams and fairy-tale endings, and you simply have a man who is no longer dating a woman he thought might be the one. Today you have uncovered the truth, and the truth frees you from all the emotional burdens that have weighed you down for far too long. Does that make sense now?"

It not only made sense, but he stood up and gave me a hug!

"Strange how easy it is to get ourselves all worked up over nothing, isn't it?" he said as he walked to his car.

Making sense of our sorrows and setbacks includes understanding how the mind operates, often quite independently from what is best for us. Dreadful, upsetting, and deeply disturbing thoughts can take root in our minds until they take over as a pesky patch of weeds we can't get rid of. And before long, we can think of nothing else and are consumed by the emotional burdens they produce. Catching stressful thoughts before they take root is the key to avoiding so much of the pain and misery that afflicts the best of us.

There's likely a lot about Rob's story that you can relate with. Your circumstances may differ, but most of us are afflicted by troublesome feelings that flow from how we think about a current circumstance or person. A simple three-part exercise can help you get to the bottom of what disturbs you.

1. Write down your thoughts about what disturbs you the most right now. Be honest and free with your thoughts. Get them out

of your head, where they get all tangled up, and put them onto the paper in front of you, where they can be examined. Focus on what you think of the situation, the people involved, the flow of events from the beginning to now, and so on.

2. Now review what you've written and identify 3–5 key thoughts or themes that are typical of what you currently think. For Rob these were: I've lost the perfect woman, I'll never find another one like her, my life is over, and so on. With your key disturbing thoughts before you to clearly see and examine, ask yourself a few questions. First, "Is this really true?" This question appears absurd. If we think something, then of course it's true, right? Not necessarily. Rob learned that in spite of what he had thought for weeks, he had in fact not lost the perfect woman for him. It may be helpful to ask a similar question with a little more teeth. "Can I know for certain that this is true? Am I sure? Can I be positive?" If you still think the thought is true, then move on to the next question, which is "And it means _____." Whether a thought is true or not is less important than what you think it *means*. Write out what you think it means and then circle back to the original questions. "Is this really true? Can I really know that it means what I have concluded?" Do this exercise for all 3–5 key disturbing thoughts.

3. Now explore each thought in another way. Rob honestly thought he had lost the perfect woman. His alternate and opposite thought was "I haven't lost the perfect woman at all." Now return to the same questions as above. Is this reverse statement as true or valid as your disturbing thought? Is it possible that this is more true than what you first believed? As you ask these questions of very different thoughts from those that disturb you, notice the shift in your feelings. If your thoughts change from stressful to peaceful, so will your feelings. You may discover, as did Rob, that a simple change of a few stressful thoughts changes the way the entire world appears. All of this proves once more that we are not actually disturbed by what happens to us but by the thoughts we have about what happens. A more profound insight is difficult to find![3]

Notes

1. Epictetus, http://en.wikipedia.org/wiki/Epictetus.
2. Ibid.
3. Adapted from Byron Katie, *Loving What Is* (San Bruno, California: Audio Literature, 2002), book on CD; see also Byron Katie, *Loving What Is: Four Questions That Can Change Your Life* (New York: Random House, 2002).

MAKING MEANING

On the same day, at exactly the same time, in the same company, three friends—Mike, Chad, and Brandon—lost their jobs. The men had similar backgrounds, professional experience and skill levels, and were well liked in the respective divisions of the organization. Each was outgoing, interested in helping people, and found a great deal of satisfaction helping others succeed. Rumors of company downsizing had drifted through the organization, but nobody had taken them seriously, including Mike, Chad, and Brandon. They felt their jobs were secure because they were making important contributions to sales—the sacrosanct "bottom line" of most organizations.

Then one day, like a bombshell, it all came crashing down. At the exact time, across three time zones, each man was ushered into his boss's office where an HR executive from headquarters told them that in spite of their good work and terrific performance, they were being let go. Five minutes before, each man was gainfully employed doing something they each loved. Suddenly, however, all of that changed. After a few hours to collect their things, the three men drove home to very similar lives in the suburbs.

Within the hour, the three friends were on the phone with one another comparing notes. Their experiences were identical—a short announcement that they were no longer employed, details of the severance, and assurance that each would be receiving further details from headquarters.

But this is where the similarities ended. All had lost their job, all were unemployed and would need to find another job, and all would receive the same package on their departure. The days that followed this initial announcement would reveal vast differences in how each man responded to the news. Their story underscores an important principle for each of us as we struggle to make sense of our own setbacks and negative surprises.

As they talked, only hours after learning the news, Chad joked, "I was looking for a job when I found this one." That afternoon he began making calls to old colleagues, head hunters, and former employers. He had kept his network active in case something like this ever happened. Within a month he had a new job at a higher level, making more money than he before. The downsizing experience made barely a ripple in his life and career. Unaffected by the experience, Chad accepted the news, created a plan, and pressed forward with few complaints.

Though initially stunned by the news, Mike took a week off to be with his family and think things through. For years his dad and brother had wanted him to move home and help run the thriving family furniture business. But Mike had bigger dreams and wanted to work in corporate America. This was the second time he had been through a downsizing in five years, and after talking things through with his wife, he decided to return to the family business. He joked to his two friends, "At least in my family's business the only person who can downsize me is my dad—and he needs me too much to ever do that. Besides, cutting me off would put a damper on family reunions." Within weeks he had sold his house in Dallas and moved home to New Jersey.

Then there was Brandon. Of the three, he had been with the company the longest. Flamboyant and a bit unpredictable, people loved him. He was more comic than corporate citizen, and that's what people liked the most. He was a fun guy, with a down-to-earth perspective on business. He prided himself on making good friends with his clients, and the news of his departure was hard on everyone who knew him. But this negative surprise was most difficult for Brandon. Initially he was angry and threatened to sue the company for violating his employment agreement. He was on the phone with company lawyers threatening all kinds of repercussions if they went through with this illegal decision. He soon learned that there was no legal case and was forced to drop the issue. He felt betrayed, mistreated, and lied to by the very people he had trusted for so long. He was angry, bitter, but most of all terrified and swamped with anxiety and fear. Three months after losing his job, Brandon still sat at home in front of the TV in a daze. He had lost interest in everything, including his family. But worst of all, he lost all hope that he could ever find another job and put his career back together. His wife grew increasingly concerned as day after day Brandon sunk deeper and deeper into despair. She encouraged him to see a therapist, but he refused. The company had even offered to pay for an outplacement service to help him locate another job, but he was unwilling to meet with them. To his concerned wife, it seemed that Brandon's stubbornness was his way of getting even for what the company had done to him.

Finally Brandon landed an interview with the aid of a recruiter at his brother's company. He had listed Chad and Mike as references the company could call. One day, nearly six months after the downsizing experience, Mike received a call. The man on the line said he had interviewed Brandon and had a few questions about him that perhaps Mike could help answer. Mike was thrilled to be of any assistance he could and excited that Brandon was actually looking for work again.

"I'm wondering if I can ask you a couple questions about Brandon," said the recruiter. "This isn't going very well," he admitted. "I'm concerned about Brandon, and I'm wondering if you can help me better understand what's happening with him."

"I'm happy to help any way I can," said Mike, curious about what he was about to hear.

"As you may know," continued the recruiter, "since losing his job, he has lost his desire to work. I've sent him on several interviews and he has flopped. The clients find him a bit moody, and he seems to lack interest in the job. He openly tells others how his previous company wronged him by laying him off a month before Christmas. I'm not sure if I can help him. That's why I called to see if you had any suggestions."

This conversation and subsequent visits with Brandon's wife confirmed what Mike most feared. He could see that Brandon was caught in a downward spiral. Depressed and hopeless, the job interviews he did secure were a disaster. The more he interviewed and failed, the more convinced he was that he would never find another job—which only added to his despair. Nearly two years after the downsizing, Brandon was still not working except for a part-time job at his sister's car wash for minimum wage. Two years earlier he was flying high, traveling around the world as a corporate trainer, speaking to large groups who gave him standing ovations. Now he shuffled through his days with no direction, no hope, and little desire to do much more than what he was now doing. A year into his car wash job, his wife of seven years could take it no more and filed for divorce. Not surprisingly, for Brandon her departure proved beyond any doubt that he was as worthless as he believed. Brandon was single-handedly destroying everything he cared for in life. His fall began with one experience, which became the detonator that destroyed his entire life. The three-year aftershocks could all be traced back to one day when the earth shook beneath him and the effect was devastating.

Here is a man who kept getting in his own way. His reaction to one event cast a shadow over his entire life, single-handedly dragging him deeper and deeper into a dark hole from which he could not easily escape. Worse than what happened to Brandon was his complete lack of awareness about why life had become so difficult. Unaware of his stressful and self-defeating thoughts, he became locked in patterns of thinking and reacting that made matters worse, not better.

Many of our most difficult experiences in life come from unwanted circumstances that we neither planned nor anticipated. Negative surprises, sudden reversals of fortune, or shocking news of another's downfall are nearly impossible to believe. Each of us, no matter who we are, will encounter circumstances in life that require our response. Indeed, learning to respond to adverse circumstances is a primary reason for coming to earth. We are here to prove two things to ourselves and Father in Heaven: First, that we will keep His commandments at all times and in all places; and second, that our circumstances will have no power over us. By our God-given agency, we have the power to choose at all times. As Father Lehi put it, we are here to either "act" or "be acted upon" (2 Nephi 2:14). What will we do when difficult circumstances come our way? How will we respond? What effect will our difficulties have on us, now and in the future?

The eminent Christian philosopher James Allen observed, "If circumstances had the power to bless or harm, they would bless and harm all men alike, but the fact that the same circumstances will be alike good and bad to different souls proves that the good or bad is not in the circumstance, but only in the mind of him that encounters it."[1]

This insight contains several crucial truths for making sense of life's difficult circumstances and retaining our power over them. First, Allen reminds us that circumstances, in and of themselves, have no power over us. They cannot depress us, anger us, ruin our day, or put us in a bad mood. He isn't saying that some circumstances are not hard—for they are. Many are real, requiring faith and determination to resist the undertow of a negative circumstance. We know that it is not our circumstances that have power because people can pass through identical circumstances and come out of them as differently as did Mike, Chad, and Brandon. If circumstances had power over us and our reactions and quality of life, then the three men who were downsized in the same way, on the same day, and at the same time, would have all reacted the same way. They didn't. Their reactions ran the gamut from excitement about the next opportunity to deep discouragement and depression on the other. The differences were in the men, and in their reaction to what happened, not in the downsizing situation or circumstance.

When engulfed by a difficult trial, we can rarely see this radiant truth. Most people are convinced that they feel as they do because of what has happened to them. "I was on the top of the world one day. Then I lost my job, and my world came crashing down. How can you tell me that losing my job isn't the reason I feel so lost and anxious?" It's clear that difficult, unexpected circumstances make us think we have lost control over our lives and our emotions. This is what Brandon believed. When his job ended, so did his confidence that he could ever find another job. His thoughts became dark, his moods even darker, and hope was utterly shattered. And yet two other men, facing identical circumstances, experienced none of what Brandon did.

When your own sore trials come, as they surely will, how will you respond? What will you think? How will you react? Will your thoughts be positive? Will you respond in productive ways or negative, self-defeating counterproductive ways? And most important of all, who but you gets to answer such significant questions? Who else but you gets to decide how an experience will impact you at the point it occurs and in the months and years that follow? Who but you is permitted to write the rest of the story?

People like Brandon have little idea the role they play in their ongoing difficulties. They have no idea that they are choosing their response to a circumstance. Nor do they see that their reaction to a circumstance, not the specific circumstance, causes their emotional burdens. When I am talking with someone who shares their list of burdens, I listen as patiently as I can and then ask them a few questions.

"Who gets to decide what will happen next for you? Who decides how your life will be next week or next year? Who's really in charge here?"

They are usually unprepared for this. "What do you mean who gets to decide? Of course I get to decide. It's my life."

"Well then, decide. Grab the wheel of your life and start steering it in the direction you want to go. Don't allow setbacks, negative surprises, or shocking experiences to dictate how your life will be. You make the call—always have and always will."

James Allen wrote, "You are swayed by circumstances because you have not a right understanding of the nature, use, and power of thought."[2]

Let's return to Mike, Chad, and Brandon for a moment. One day each man learned that he no longer had a job with his present company. Thus the three different men faced, in that moment, identical circumstances. Each was married with kids, each was in his thirties, and each had talent to take to another company. But in the hours and days that followed, important differences began to manifest themselves. These differences lay in the thoughts, stories, and beliefs each man had about that experience. To build on James Allen's insight, the only real but important difference between Brandon and his two friends is very simple. Brandon had a thought or series of thoughts that Mike and Chad simply didn't have. His thoughts were negative. He took the news personally and believed he could not easily recover from this setback. Mike and Chad either didn't have such thoughts at all or if they did, they quickly replaced these thoughts with more productive thoughts that empowered them to move forward in spite of this unexpected experience. For Brandon, one stressful, negative thought became the trigger for a long line of painful experiences. It all began with a single thought that wasn't even true. But because he believed it was true, he was swallowed up by the stress and emotional turbulence it produced.

This is a stunning truth with huge implications—to realize that in any circumstance in life, we alone determine how it will affect us, for good or ill. And how do we do this? Simply by how we think about the experience, by the thoughts that rise up in our heads and that we almost always believe are true. Brandon wasn't depressed because of losing a job. He simply thought he was, and this thought left him powerless once his job was gone. Brandon always thought it was his job that made him happy and feel successful, and once his job had been erased off a company's organization chart, then he could do nothing but lament over what he once had. Whenever we think our dark feelings are caused by circumstances or other people, we have unwittingly handed over all our power to something external. Feelings of hopelessness and helplessness arise from the thoughts we have about what has happened, and the belief that there is no other way to think about our troubling situation than the way we do.

Let's be clear. Stern, sad, unwanted circumstances can affect us. It is normal to be saddened by the passing of a friend, the loss of a job, or a scary diagnosis. These can be jarring and remind us that we are not in control of what happens around us and that life is very uncertain. Initial sadness or disbelief is normal. But the circumstance has no real power. It's simply an event that really means nothing until we make it mean something. And how do we do this? We infuse meaning into a meaningless experience. Inside our heads we concoct a stressful story about the circumstance, what it means, and how it will affect us, and then we believe that story. But in fact, the stressful story we invent is fictional, made up to make sense of what has happened.

"What are you suggesting?" you may protest. "I don't invent stories in my head when something bad happens. That would be crazy."

Yes, it would be crazy, but you do it all the time whether you like it or not—and whether you believe it or not.

If the circumstance has no power, all the power rests with us. And what can we do with this power? We can craft any story we choose. We can make our circumstances mean whatever we like. It's not like there is one true story and a hundred false ones. We make them mean whatever we say they mean! We can view a job loss as a great blessing that allows us to do all the things we've always wanted to do but never had time to before. Or we can make it mean something dark and stressful, inventing a story of fear, defeat, and depressing uncertainty in the future. We are given one hundred percent of the power over any circumstance in life. The circumstance has zero power. So if we have all the power to make it mean whatever we desire and prefer, then why not make it mean something positive, uplifting, and motivating? If we really do get to say what any experience means, and we do, why not say something like, "This is a good thing. I'm glad this happened because I know that it will lead to something better. I will learn what I've always wanted to learn but didn't know how to learn it. This is a very good thing for me and those I love."

You may be thinking, "Hey, you're just making that up! You have no idea if that's really true. It might be a terrible tragedy, and you're looking at it like its all good."

Very true, and that's the point. An experience means whatever we say it means. If we say it is a terrible tragedy and that it has power to depress us, then it will. If we say it's a good thing that will teach us needed lessons and lead us in a positive direction, then it will. Thus we empower any experience with whatever impact we choose. It has no power until we infuse power into it by the way we view it, by the interpretation we give it, and by what we make the experience mean. That's the kind of power you have as you face and overcome any negative circumstance in life.

Here are a few suggestions for putting your personal power to use.

1. Jot down on paper the most difficult circumstance you currently face in any area of your life. If you have more than one, list all you can think of that you feel are difficult, stressful, worrisome, or hard.

2. What would you like each circumstance to mean? For each circumstance, describe how you would like it to be, what good you would like to see come from it, and so on. You are finishing the sentence "This means that _____." Remember that you, and you alone, get to say what a given circumstance means. You were planning to go on a mission and now you can't for health reasons. What will you make it mean? You were engaged, and he broke it off for no good reason. What will you make it mean? You and your spouse were looking forward to spending your retirement together but she died last year of breast cancer. What will you make this mean?

When you face a difficult circumstance, no matter what it is, examine what you are currently making it mean—and then make it mean something else. You have the power. Your circumstances have no power. As a result, you get to say what a circumstance means and how it will affect you, not the circumstance itself.

At all times, remember this one glittering truth. Life supplies the circumstance, you supply the meaning. Part of life is our ability to choose our reaction to any and all circumstances. A friend of mine has a son who was sent to jail for committing a felony. He was guilty and had to serve his time. But when he left, I reminded him of this truth. "You get to say what all of this means from right now on. Going to jail means whatever you think it means. What you think it says about you is all crafted inside your own head. It only means what you make it mean. You are in charge of your life, not this unfortunate event."

He has now served his time and is a stronger, more committed man than ever. He made it mean that he had a chance to prove to himself, his family, and God what he was really made of, what he would do with this experience. He used his power to turn a difficult circumstance into a major stepping stone in his life. Let us all do the same.

Notes

1. James Allen, http://jamesallenlibrary.com/from-poverty-to-power-the-world-a-reflex-of-mental-states.html. See also James Allen, *The Path of Prosperity* (New York: SoHo Books, 2010).
2. Ibid.

Avoiding the Guilt Trap

Friends and family jokingly refer to Jennie as the "guilt queen." Almost everything makes her feel guilty. But guilt rarely comes calling alone. Usually stress, anxiety, and confusion accompany it. Jennie often feels trapped by a moral dilemma feeling she "should" do two things but can, in fact, only do one. She should be more patient with her children, but they continually test her patience. When her frustration flares, as it often does, she feels guilty about losing her temper. Jennie feels caught in a constant cycle most of the time that goes from guilt to frustration to action that creates guilt. The smallest things can bring on a rush of guilty feelings. Preceding her guilty feelings are several guilt-producing thoughts that Jennie often experiences as demands or commands. Hence, she doesn't simply have a casual thought of something she should do, like call a friend, take her children to the park, or attend a former roommate's wedding one thousand miles away. The voice in her head compels her to do these things. The problem is that she often feels torn between two opposite demands. The voice in her head is constantly chattering away, as it is for all of us, but Jennie's head is awash with a plethora of "shoulds," adding undue stress to her life. For her, any experience can produce an intense inner struggle.

As more and more Jennies pop up around the Church, our leaders speak publicly about the negative consequences of guilt. They tell us repeatedly that no one can be perfect in this life, nor can anyone always do the right thing. Then they tell us to stop feeling guilty. Jennie has attended countless conferences where professionals speak of the tendency that women have to feel an overwhelming sense of guilt. But telling a guilt queen she shouldn't feel guilty is pointless. Although she doesn't realize it, a part of Jennie believes she is supposed to feel guilty—that if she doesn't feel guilty, she isn't striving for perfection. She thinks that guilt motivates her to do the right thing—that through guilt, her conscience is telling her what she should and shouldn't think, feel, and do. When her husband tells her to stop making every little thing into a moral dilemma, she feels he doesn't understand and isn't supportive. She may even think he is insensitive or callous to her present moral crisis. Her stressful thoughts not only "tell" her how she should think, feel, and act but they also "tell" her that others *should* feel similarly. Jennie never considers the possibility that she is creating her own dilemmas by her either/or thinking and at times wonders why others don't wrestle with the same issues in the same way as she.

To people like Jennie, this all seems terribly complicated and feels very stressful. At times Jennie feels afflicted with a hyper-sensitive knowledge of right and wrong that places her in a "no-win" corner from which she can't escape without feeling guilty. Whatever she decides, she loses and brings upon her a string of burdensome feelings. In fact, guilt like Jennie's is not all that complicated once you understand where it originates. Simple sermons that tell us not to feel guilty are not helpful because they don't address the heart of the guilt issue. They presume that bright, intelligent, committed people who feel guilty simply need to stop feeling guilty. "It's not helpful. It makes you crazy and stressed out, so don't do it!" This advice assumes that people like Jennie are simply unaware that their guilt is making them miserable and that once they are told to stop, they'll simply stop and get back to an easier, less stressful life.

But guilt is not the result of a lack of awareness. Jennie already knows that most days she feels caught on the horns of some kind of dilemma that she doesn't enjoy but feels unable to resolve. People who love her see the pressure she puts on herself and those around her by pacing up and down in the stressful cell of yet another guilt-producing situation. They see the tension it creates in her marriage and with her children. They see the toll it takes on her joy, which is interrupted and eroded on a regular basis by feelings of guilt and Jennie's own inability to effectively resolve her feelings. But all the talk in the world does little good because in ways she doesn't really understand, Jennie thinks she is *supposed* to feel this way. It reflects her innate goodness and determination to always do the right thing in every situation. She believes, perhaps not consciously, that feeling guilty is what deeply committed and caring people always experience. It is the cross they bear in life, and there is simply no way around it.

As is true with most stressful feelings, guilt has its origin in stressful, distorted, and often completely erroneous thoughts and beliefs. Once we understand the connection between these two critical factors—guilt and erroneous thoughts—guilt makes more sense and is not as difficult to resolve as we think. No problem can be effectively resolved until the underlying cause is ascertained. The rash on your skin may be due to one of several underlying causes or a combination of factors. But the rash is merely the symptom of the problem, not the problem itself. Think how fruitless it would be for a doctor to prescribe cream for a skin rash that was actually caused by an undiagnosed food sensitivity. You could plow through buckets of skin cream and never touch the underlying cause. The rash would seem to go on forever. Similarly, incessant guilty feelings that lead to no productive end are the symptom of a problem that originates in our head. Certain thoughts, stories, and beliefs taken as true will produce feelings of guilt in anyone who entertains them. Until the habits of thought and erroneous beliefs are uncovered and replaced, guilt will persist, regardless of how many conferences Jennie attends that tell her to stop feeling guilty. Inside the pressure-packed world of Jennie's thoughts, stopping the guilt is not an option.

Earlier we noted that most people misinterpret their feelings. None do it more often and with more precision than individuals afflicted by guilt. They incorrectly interpret their feelings of guilt as proof that they must do this or that. The strength of their guilty feelings is used as evidence that what we think we should do must indeed be done. For example, some women feel intense guilt if they don't rise early in the morning to cook their children a hot breakfast before school. If they forget or for some reason can't do it one morning, they feel guilty. They *believe* that their strong feelings of guilt are proof that they must do as they feel compelled to do. The logic makes some sense but still does not serve them well. They think, "If I wasn't supposed to do this, then I wouldn't feel so guilty." Thus the way they know that they are really supposed to do one thing instead of another is by how guilty each option makes them feel. They are not guided by proven principles or values but by feelings of guilt. The stronger the guilt, the more important the given action.

Guilty thoughts are experienced as moral imperatives. Jennie thinks to herself, "I really should nurse my babies, but I hate it. It ties me down, and it's messy. I'm not positive it's all that critical to a baby's health." But her feelings of guilt, springing from what she feels she *should* do, exert intense pressure on her, in spite of her arguments for doing something else, even something she really prefers. Such individuals are constantly caught between what they want to do and what they feel they *should* or *have to* do. And why should they do it? Because their strong feelings of guilt tell them what must be done, whether they want to do so or not.

It's easy to see how these initial guilt feelings can spin into resentment. We want to do one thing but feel guilty about it, so we do what reduces our guilt rather than what we really want to do, regardless of the eventual result of our actions. The divorced father who feels guilt over his divorce and the impact on his kids overindulges them on his bimonthly visits. This reduces his guilt but is not healthy for his kids, nor their relationship with him. Before long he complains that when he gets together with his kids, they just want him to take them to fun, expensive places and spend money he doesn't have on toys, candy, and the like. The right and best thing for both father and children is trumped by excessive feelings of guilt. In time, he will likely grow resentful of his kids' unreasonable demands, and the children will feel his irritation and not understand why he is upset with them. Thus an unhealthy and unhappy pattern is set in motion all because a father was driven by feelings of guilt rather than guided by principles of effective relationships,

There is an important distinction between guilt and remorse. Genuine remorse plays a critical role in our efforts to repent and improve whereas guilt serves no positive purpose. Unhealthy guilt, as we've been discussing, is the way we feel when we hold and ruminate on the following kinds of thoughts.

- I have done something I shouldn't have done or failed to do what I should have done.
- I have fallen short of the kind of person I am supposed to be.
- I have failed to live up to standards I deeply believe in.

When we impose unrealistic standards of behavior on ourselves, we will fall short. And when we do, we will feel guilty. This is a very common trap for new mothers. They have a set of self-imposed standards about how they are supposed to think, feel, and act when they have a baby. I heard one new mother say, "I'm supposed to love being a mom all the time. I should never want to leave my baby to go to the gym or take a class. But at times I just want to get away. When I do, I feel so guilty." This woman feels guilty because she doesn't feel the way she thinks she is *supposed* to feel. Such patterns of thought generate feelings of guilt, and the unrealistic standards we impose on ourselves are never considered. The new mother feels caught in a dilemma she can never resolve since she has no idea what has put her in the stressful trap that ensnares her. The possibility that she unwittingly put herself in this trap never crosses her mind.

We sometimes think that when we fall short of some moral standard that we *believe* good people almost always attain, it means we are bad people. We misinterpret guilt as a sign of our diminished value or innate goodness. People with nagging feelings of guilt often wrestle with deep insecurities. After all, how can you feel good about yourself when you feel guilty? And how can you feel God's love if you're preoccupied with guilty feelings that you constantly misinterpret? This sad cycle begins when we impose impractical standards on ourselves, fail to meet them, and then judge ourselves because we have fallen short. "If I was really a good person, I would have done what I failed to do," is the conclusion that generates tremendous guilt. Then to add insult to injury, we conclude, "If I was the kind of person I know I should be, I wouldn't feel this way."

When caught in these self-defeating cycles we feel there is no escape. Caught on the horns of a difficult dilemma, we conclude that no matter what we do, we are failing to do what we *should* do. Our guilt is compounded by our lack of ability to resolve what afflicts us. We feel guilty so we try to do something to alleviate our guilty feelings, often falling short and thereby deepening our guilt. Sometimes it is virtually impossible for us to do what we think we should. For example, Jennie just received an invitation to a former college roommate's wedding reception halfway across the country. Her first thought? "I really should go because she is a good friend and she came to my reception." When her husband points out the impossibility of traveling so far to attend a one-hour wedding, Jennie's guilt only intensifies.

Even the thought of not going triggers further guilt, for now she feels like she is making excuses for what she believes she *must* do. And how does her husband's argument sound to Jennie? He is insensitive, doesn't understand, and isn't supportive. Undaunted, she scours the web, looking for a good airfare and cheap hotel. But after hours of trying, she finally realizes that attending the wedding is impossible. And what does this cause her to feel? You can now predict because you can see the pattern in Jennie's guilt-ridden life. She feels bad for not being able to work it out. Somewhere in her frenzied stressed-out mind is the thought, *If I was really a good friend, I'd make this work.* Every time she thinks of this friend or sees her in the future, these feelings of guilt rush back, causing her to apologize and feel bad for not doing what she felt she needed to do. Her twisted reasoning controls her emotional life and creates a stream of stress for Jennie and those who love her.

It's not unusual for guilt-ridden individuals to also feel shame and even depression. It all depends on their thinking and the negative assumptions they make. Jennie is a classic example. Because she didn't attend her friend's wedding even though her friend attended hers, Jennie feels inferior. "I am not the kind of friend I should be. If I were, I would find a way. I would make it work." In addition to intense guilt, Jennie feels ashamed and fearful of others finding out. "If others found out what I did, they would look down on me." This thought leads to shame. "I'm in danger of retaliation or punishment from people or God." This thought provokes anxiety. The thought that a close friend would think less of her causes Jennie to feel bad. But because she blames herself, she feels shame for not doing what *she felt* she should have done. Having failed, she beats herself up for weeks after, adding persecution to her burdensome feelings of guilt.

It's easy to see how people like Jennie become ensnared in a trap from which they cannot easily escape. Unaware of how their distorted thinking makes them feel, they struggle against their head and heart, in a constant battle between what they feel they *should* do and what is physically possible. When we are out of touch with our own stressful thinking, distorted beliefs, and faulty assumptions, we become enslaved to stressful emotions that afflict us and undermine our peace.

Throughout this volume, we will revisit a central theme at the heart of making sense of our trials, setbacks, and surprises. Stressful, burdensome feelings reflect stressful, distorted thinking. The voices in our heads and the stream of automatic thoughts they produce can be our worst enemies. God is not causing us to suffer, others are not making us angry, and people and circumstances are not the source of our stress. The best news of all is that we alone are responsible; we are creating most of our suffering. This is painfully clear when guilt and shame are involved. People like Jennie are afflicted with distorted thoughts and beliefs they think are true and then act upon this belief. Outsiders can see that people like Jennie are drowning in negative, self-defeating thoughts that they think are true but which others can see are irrational and counterproductive.

GUILT AND REMORSE

It's helpful to distinguish the kind of guilt we have been talking about and healthy remorse. Guilt is a disorder of thought and twisted logic spilling over into our moods and feelings. As such it can't be resolved, since we are absolutely convinced of the accuracy of our thinking, which is confirmed by our feelings. Guilt serves no productive purpose in our life and leads nowhere, as we have illustrated above. Guilt includes a negative judgment of self, thus eroding a sense of worth and worthiness. People who feel a regular dose of guilt will also struggle with self-confidence since they are caught so often in moral dilemmas created by their thoughts.

On the other hand, remorse stems from the clear awareness that you have willfully acted in a hurtful manner toward yourself or another person, which violates your personal and ethical standards. You feel that being kind and caring is what Christ would have you do. Expressing uncalled for displeasure toward a child or saying something hurtful to a friend may cause understandable remorse. This is not an emotion flowing from a twisted thought. It is, however, a lapse between what we want to be and who we are, in a given situation. We want to be patient and we're not. We want to stop arguing with our teenager, but we keep getting into it, making the relationship even more corrosive. We make a concerted commitment to study our scriptures more often and after three months we realize we have made little, if any, progress toward this new goal. We behave below standards we agree to and genuinely desire to follow. Remorse naturally follows.

Remorse also differs from guilt in another important respect. Guilt implies that you are inherently bad, evil, or immoral. Remorse is the awareness that we have broken our agreements with self or others, and we need to realign ourselves, repent, and get back on track. Remorse or regret is directed toward changing how we think and behave. Guilt, on the other hand, is directed inward toward the self through judgment and blame—chastising ourselves for what we have done or failed to do.

Guilt is a strong negative emotion that arises from three primary distortions in our thinking—magnification, labeling, and personalizing. When Jennie realizes she can't attend her friend's wedding, she magnifies the importance of the problem. She begins thinking that attending the wedding is far more critical than it actually is. She magnifies a simple wedding invitation into a major dilemma, affecting her and everyone close to her. Of course, if this has been a habit of thought most of her life, she is blind to how she magnifies a multitude of daily "shoulds," leaving her engulfed in stressful, burdensome feelings.

Moreover, guilt usually arises when we think we have done something wrong. For Jennie it was as simple as not attending a friend's wedding. Nothing her husband could say could change the guilt she felt for weeks afterward. She should have gone but didn't. This transgression made Jennie anxious about seeing her friend in the future.

When we fall short of unrealistically high standards, we often label ourselves in negative ways. "I'm such a bad mother," says the woman whose kids are always crying at church. A simple church meeting can become a highly stressful experience if a parent thinks, "Kids are supposed to be quiet," and "If I was a good parent I would do a better job at controlling my kids." Thus we magnify what is happening, label ourselves in negative ways and personalize the entire experience.

When we personalize a situation, we assume responsibility for something we didn't cause. For instance, you say something to a friend, and he becomes upset and defensive. You take it personally and feel that you caused his reaction, which makes you "feel bad," meaning you feel responsible and guilty. Or because your kids were noisy in church you conclude that you ruined the meeting for everyone else. The truth is your kids were noisy along with all the other children in church. Also, you did not ruin anything. And how could you really know if you ruined another person's experience? The absurd conclusion flows from a string of magnifications, labelings, and personalizations—all distorted, stressful thought patterns that generate a host of stressful feelings.

Unrealistic "should" statements lie at the center of guilty feelings. Such statements and their underlying beliefs set us up for failure by establishing impossible standards of thought and behavior. Some people unrealistically think they should be happy at all times. This rigid credo drives their every waking moment. So what do we conclude when we are unhappy, stressed out, or upset? We label ourselves as failures, creating both guilt and shame. Rigid, unrealistic standards of what we should and should not think, feel, and do are a ticking time bomb in our emotional life. So much emotional pain comes from holding impossible beliefs, completely impractical "shoulds," that we can never consistently attain. No wonder we hear our leaders often speak of "incremental improvement" one step at a time, line upon line, with a season for everything rather than perfection by Monday morning.

Clearly, there is no shortage of guilt-ridden people these days. Between scriptural injunctions to "be perfect," self-imposed unrealistic expectations, and various societal pressures to "have it all," stressful feelings of guilt abound. I have attempted in this chapter to explain where those feelings come from and to make the important connection between mental distortions and the guilty feelings they produce. Legitimate remorse that leads to repentance is always necessary to restore us to the peace of Christ. But there is no positive, productive purpose for guilt. It leads nowhere, causes many of our emotional burdens, and can easily be avoided by learning to see things clearly and accurately. Without question or debate, mental distortions create stressful feelings. In fact, our negative feelings signal that something in our thinking is awry. As I have said in other chapters, we must always keep in mind that thoughts are just things, and things can change. We are not our thoughts. Thoughts—uplifting *and* stressful—arise unbidden, incessantly and automatically from out of nowhere. To date there has been no proven method for controlling stressful thoughts, although we can certainly become more aware of how our thoughts generate negative and stressful feelings.

Keep in mind, there are essentially only two ways to go through life: stressfully or peacefully. Any time you feel stressful emotions, interpret them for what they actually are and be aware of what they are telling you. Just as thoughts of genuine love cannot produce stress, negative stressful thoughts will only produce anxiety and various troublesome emotions. But keep in mind that the presence of strong negative feelings proves only one thing for certain. Inside your head, you have attached to thoughts that are not true, creating intense inner turmoil. Allow your stressful feelings to lead you back upstream to the thoughts from which they naturally flow. Now is the time to rid yourself of the toxic emotions of guilt and shame before they inflict any more emotional or spiritual damage.

Before I offer a few suggestions, first I have a caveat. In all likelihood, your habits of thought that lead to regular feelings of guilt and shame have been with you for a long time. They will not go away easily. You have been thinking in stressful, distorted ways most of your life and can't imagine thinking any other way. Guilt is a devilish emotion, from which flow devilish ideas. If you are one who easily feels guilty, you may even feel a twinge of guilt when you engage in exercises designed to reduce or eliminate stressful, non-productive guilt. You likely cling to a twisted, erroneous belief that says, "I'm supposed to feel guilty. If I don't feel some guilt, that would be dangerous, and I wouldn't be normal." Keep in mind what I've said about guilt as opposed to honest remorse. This is an important distinction that you must always keep in mind.

Strange as it may seem, a part of you doesn't want to let go of your guilty feelings. You may erroneously think you are supposed to feel guilty. You may presume that without guilt you would drift from strong moral standards and fail to know how to direct your life. You only think this way because it's the way you have been thinking for a long time. You have given your agency away to the much stronger feelings of guilt. Sadly, some individuals decide what is right or wrong based on how guilty they feel. This too is merely another thought you believe is true. Look carefully at the emotional outcomes of such distorted thinking and you'll see how self-defeating it can be.

Why would you cling to anything that makes you unhappy and emotionally upset? This is not the Lord's way. Distorted thoughts never lead to peace and happiness. In fact quite the opposite is true. If we often feel guilty, confused, and anxious, can these feelings really be coming from God? Or could they simply be untrue thoughts and beliefs you have had for a long time that you think are true? Whenever we believe thoughts that are untrue for us, we will always bring upon ourselves various stressful and confusing feelings. Thus dispelling false ideas we once believed true is the key to ridding ourselves of the negative effects of guilt and shame.

Here are a few ideas for how to begin the process of changing your thoughts to create more productive outcomes.

1. When you feel guilty, stop what you're doing and write down your thoughts. If it's impossible to stop at that moment, record your thoughts as soon as you can. Guilt and shame originate in your thinking, so begin here. Our negative feelings are easy to notice because they are strong and stressful. We're less in touch with our thoughts, in part because they arise so quickly and automatically. After years of running down the same old mental ruts, your thoughts have probably settled into negative patterns you know far too well—but they are making you crazy.

2. For each thought, identify the *should* or *shouldn't* statements that are either obvious or implicit. Behind guilt and shame are various thoughts of things we *should* think, feel, and do. "I should be a better provider for my family. I shouldn't get upset with my kids as much as I do. I really need to be a better friend." Behind every guilty feeling is a thought of what you *should* do. Uncover it and write it down.

3. For each *should* statement, ask a few questions to investigate the validity of your thoughts.

   a) How do I know I should? What makes me think this is true? How do I know it's really true?

   b) Where's my proof? Just because we think that something is true, doesn't make it true. So where is your proof that this thought is true?

   c) How do you treat yourself when you believe this thought? How do you treat others? Where did this thought originate? How long have you believed this thought? How does it affect you today and in the past?

Far too many of us have lived with guilt much too long. Now is the time to inquire into the various thinking errors that cause these toxic emotions. It is time for the burden of guilt to be lifted once and for all. Like a heavy bag of rocks, it does nothing more than weigh you down in various areas of life, robbing you of the joy you seek and the peace the Savior wants you to experience. The only thing that stands between you and increased peace and joy is changing your mind, which is not as daunting as you might think.

ME? JUDGE?

Early in my career I worked as a marriage and family therapist. About a month into the job, I discovered that I mostly refereed fights. The primary reason people came to my office was that conflict, contention, and frustration had reached an unacceptable level. Something needed to change.

The most memorable experience I had in these early days was a series of conversations with a couple who had been married for thirty years. After only a few minutes, I could tell that twenty-nine of their thirty years together had been dissatisfying for both husband and wife. By comparison, I had been married less than a year and was blissfully happy, while they had been together for nearly a third of a of century and were miserable. To better understand trials and tribulation, we must understand how we become entangled in stressful relationships and why we can't break free of painful patterns once they begin. Understanding how we get into these painful situations and how we get stuck in them is crucial, and most people, in and out of the Church, have no idea how it happens. Many *think* they know, but it's the way they think about themselves and others with whom they quarrel that keeps them locked in deeply painful patterns.

My first meeting with this couple I mentioned earlier was intriguing, to say the least. My secretary knocked on my door and told me they were ready to see me, and I ushered them into my office. Jolene walked in and took a seat, but Ted, her husband, motioned for me to come out into the hall.

"How much time will you need with my wife?" he asked.

I was genuinely puzzled by the question. "What do you mean?" I asked. "Aren't you staying?"

He patted me on the shoulder in a condescending way and said, "Yes, I'm sure most couples are seen together, but that won't be necessary for us. Jolene has several serious emotional problems that need to be addressed and that don't involve me. So I'll be back in about an hour to pick her up." In that moment I felt more like a car mechanic talking to a customer about his old Ford that wasn't running very well. It was as if Ted had said, "Give her a good tune up, tighten up any loose nuts, and give me a call when you're done." After his little speech, he turned to walk away.

I had been taught by one of the best marriage therapists around that marriage counseling must involve both husband and wife. Emboldened by this knowledge, I called him back.

"I get the feeling you have never done marriage counseling before. Is that right?" I asked, determined to get him to stay—or at least understand the consequences of cutting himself out of the process.

"No, I've never done this before, and I understand what you're trying to do, but it really is unnecessary," he answered with no attempt to apologize. "In reality, this isn't marriage counseling. It's really just for my wife who needs a lot of individual therapy."

"But, Ted," I persisted, "I need your input to better understand what's happening between you and your wife. Don't her emotional challenges affect you in a lot of ways?"

"Of course," he said flatly.

"Then that's important to me. I need to hear your perspective as well as your wife's. I can't really help her with her difficulties without having you involved. It simply won't work."

With a heavy sigh as if to say, "I have no idea how to get out of this without looking like a jerk," he relented. I shall never forget what happened next. I learned that Ted was a former colonel in the military and had recently retired after an illustrious career. I only learned this because he told me that he had been decorated with several medals, had two tours of duty overseas, and dropped the names of several famous people he said were his friends. Had I not stopped him, I think he could have gone for hours talking about himself.

Turning to Jolene, I asked about her life and background. While he was brusque and loquacious, she was quiet and quite timid. Together they had four grown children, all reportedly doing well.

"So, tell me, what's happening in your marriage right now that brings you into marriage therapy?"

Jolene started to talk, but Ted instantly cut her off. In the next few minutes, I witnessed a pattern that had likely been their style of interacting through most of their marriage. He was clearly the commander in charge, and she was his obedient junior officer. I watched him browbeat and belittle her in front of me, with no awareness of the powerful and crystal-clear message he was sending about himself. She would try to answer my questions from her point of view, and he interrupted with what he felt was a better description of what was *really* happening. It was as if he was saying to her, "Listen, Jolene, when Randy wants your opinion, *I'll* give it to him."

Finally I interrupted his arrogant pontification and asked, "Is this the way things usually happen with the two of you? Is this how it usually goes?" She lowered her head and started to quietly cry. He looked at her with disdain and didn't bother to answer my question. But soon he was back on track, telling me that he didn't need to be part of the therapy and that I should focus my attention on his wife. Ted told me, "I think it's pretty clear that she's upset and has some emotional problems. I have nothing to do with this." And with that, he got up and walked out of my office, refusing to return a second time.

How would these two unhappy individuals make sense of their challenges and the emotional burdens they experienced? The answer seems fairly simple, at least to each of the individuals involved. He would judge her as frail, indecisive, and weak. She would judge him as a verbally abusive, overbearing brute, a self-righteous prig who blamed her for all their marital problems, and felt that he was a victim of her deep insecurities. Each would feel justified making such harsh judgments of their spouse because of how they are being treated. Both sides feel innocent and right while insisting that the other person is guilty and wrong. Ironically this was a couple active in the Church who were serving a part-time mission. They had raised their children in the Church and had been married in the temple thirty years earlier. Despite these external signs of success, within their hearts and between one another, they were awash with blame and resentment of the other, easily justifying their judgments of the other by how they were being treated.

The purpose in this chapter is not to take sides, decide who was more wrong and less right, and award points to the winner. Instead I'm asking a very different question and have a much more important purpose in mind. We can easily see the "tit for tat" pattern that develops in most relationships. He is mean, so she is afraid to talk, and then he blames her for being indecisive. And because of his angry accusations, she feels more insecure. Sadly, this is a typical pattern in relationships characterized by conflict and unhappiness.

In this chapter we're asking a different question. How do we become the kind of people who create troubling interactions with others? What happens to us when we get caught in negative patterns with others? How do we justify mistreating others when we know better? Finding fault, criticizing, blaming, and self-excusing become normal reactions to those with whom we contend. Why? If we are committed to being Christlike "at all times and in all places," how are we transformed into such devilish creatures? And once this nasty transformation occurs, how do we explain it, justify it, and somehow make it acceptable inside our own minds?

In the days that followed my initial meeting with Ted and Jolene, I reflected further on their pattern of interaction with one another. The negative patterns they employed left each party feeling mistreated and innocent. Thus, with nobody willing to take responsibility, they had become locked in a never-ending stalemate. Neither could see the part he or she played in how the relationship was going. And so, with all the blame laid at the feet of the other, both felt judged and blamed, which indeed, they were. Jolene blamed Ted for his harsh mistreatment, and Ted blamed her for being so passive, "forcing" him to treat her as he did. We can easily predict that she would say something like, "Well, if you wouldn't treat me so roughly and weren't so critical of everything I said and did, maybe I wouldn't be so passive and afraid to act." You can see the endless cycle of "attack and defend" they had fallen into—without help they would never escape.

I called Ted and asked if he would meet me alone to discuss their challenges. He enthusiastically agreed, which didn't surprise me. He presumed that I was going to reveal my plan for fixing his broken wife.

Two days later he strode confidently into my office with a notepad, ready to write down my suggestions for what Jolene needed to do and what he needed to know about her overhaul. He would need his pen and paper, but not for the reasons he expected.

I thanked him for coming and told him I had an exercise I'd like him to try, which I felt would be useful for him and Jolene.

"But Jolene's not here" he said a bit surprised. "Don't we need her if we're going to do an exercise together?"

"Not this time, Ted," I answered. "This one's all about you. But you'll like it because I'm going to let you do what you do so easily and naturally, that you probably don't even know you're doing it." He looked up at me wondering where I was going with this.

"Pull out that notepad and pen you brought," I continued. "I'd like you to write down your answers to a few questions. It's obvious to me that you feel Jolene is the cause of all your marital problems. It's also clear that in many ways she drives you crazy and frustrates you to no end." He looked at me and smiled as if finally somebody else could see what he had to live with day after day.

"Your job in this exercise is simple. I want you to judge your wife." I turned to my whiteboard behind my desk where I had written several questions. "Here are some questions to get you started. Let me give you a few guidelines. First and most important, be totally honest. Don't try to be nice or downplay or minimize Jolene's weaknesses or how you feel about her. Get down on paper every thought you have about your wife, and don't worry, I'm not going to share this with her. This is just for you and me to discuss."

On the whiteboard I had written the following questions:

1. "I am angry at Jolene because _____."
2. What do you want Jolene to change? How do you want her to act differently? "I want Jolene to _____." Make a list.
3. What advice would you give your wife? "Jolene should _____."
4. What does Jolene need to do in order for you to be happy and remain committed to this marriage? "I need Jolene to _____."
5. What do you think of Jolene? Make a list. "Jolene is _____."

He got to work answering the questions with gusto. The answers to these questions had been swirling around inside him for who knows how long. Now I was giving him complete freedom to let them fly. For his thoughts to be useful to him, however, he needed to get them out of his head and down on paper where we could examine them in a systematic way. Remember what Epictetus said: "We are disturbed not by events, but by the views which we take of them." I wanted Ted to capture his most specific and honest judgments of Jolene, for therein lay the key to his peace and to perhaps saving this tattered marriage.

I sat quietly as Ted wrote feverishly—no hesitations, no puzzlement or uncertainty about how he felt. It was obvious to me from our first session that his list of grievances against Jolene was a mile long. I was now giving him the opportunity he wanted to air those grievances before someone who, he was sure, would understand and take his side in the ongoing contention. When he was finished, he looked eagerly at me, waiting to read it. That wasn't what I wanted to do. He needed to see how his judgments of his wife were the real cause of his emotional pain. He also needed to understand that he had been doing the very things he accused her of doing. He was about to learn firsthand the truth in the maxim "What you don't own, owns you." Ted was about to see that many of his most negative feelings came from his most negative judgments of Jolene. In truth, she didn't irritate him or make him angry or exasperate him. But embroiled in his negative interaction with her, he was blind to how his judgments of her were coming back on him. We get exactly what we give. If we give love, love returns tenfold. If we give hatred, blame, and resentment, we evoke it from others, and in so doing make ourselves and others wretched. The problem is that we can't see that we're doing this. At such times of blindness, we need to see things in an entirely new way, and usually we can't do this by ourselves. That was why I knew I needed to focus on Ted's stressful thoughts and blaming emotions. Without these Ted was a fine man. With them he was a slave to his established ways of thinking and interacting that were destroying his peace and disrupting every relationship in his life.

We didn't have to go very far before hitting the bull's eye.

"Let's review what you wrote for the first question," I said. He flipped to his first page and said,

"I am angry and frustrated with Jolene for causing so much trouble in our marriage and for making our lives so difficult and complicated.

This is the time when we should be happy and carefree, but we're in counseling because she is so stubborn and stuck in her ways."

"Okay, now let's look at what you just said and examine it for truth and accuracy. One thing I know for sure: whenever we believe something that is untrue for us, we're going to suffer. That's just how it works. So, to your first point, Jolene has caused all your marriage troubles. Let me ask you, is that really true? Sit back and think for a second on what you said. Is it really true that Jolene, all by herself, has caused all your marital problems?"

He sat back as requested and then said, "Yes, Randy, I think it's true. You wouldn't believe how hard I try to be patient with Jolene, but nothing works. In fact, I think she's getting worse every day. The more I try to get her to relax and work with me, the more rebellious and hardheaded she becomes."

"So," I went on, "Jolene should do what you want her to do. She should work with you as you say. She should try to change. Is that what you think?"

"Absolutely," he shot back. "It's clear to everyone who knows her that she needs help. She's not a strong person, and I have been a leader my whole life. If she would just try to do what I need her to do, I really think we could fix what isn't working in our marriage."

"And what do you think is broken in your marriage with Jolene?" I asked

"Well, obviously she's broken. She wasn't always like this. When we first got married, she had dreams and aspirations to go back to college and get her degree. Now she sits around the house and does nothing but blame me for standing in her way. She has lost her direction, and I'm trying to get her back on track."

"Let's return to what you wrote down. You said Jolene should listen to you and do what you say, since you are trying so hard to help her. Let me ask, is that really true? Is it true that Jolene should listen to you and take your advice as you suggest? Now, Ted, I'm not asking if you *think* this is true. I'm asking, can you know for certain, with no doubt, that Jolene should listen to you and do what you say? Is that really true?"

Given his tendency for omniscience, I awaited his rapid-fire answer. He sat back in his chair and thought about what I was asking.

"I suppose I can't know for certain that she should listen to me, but it sure would make it a lot easier for all of us if she did."

"So you think she should listen to you and do what you say, but when you think a little deeper, you realize that maybe that thought's not really true." Ted looked at me, waiting to see where I was taking this conversation.

"So here's the next question," I continued. "When you think Jolene is broken and needs to listen to you and do what you say, how do you react?"

"It makes me crazy," he answered. "I am trying my hardest in this marriage, and she isn't doing anything but hanging around the house, feeling sorry for herself. I'm the only one who's trying to get us back on track. She does nothing to help me."

"You think she isn't trying. Is that true, Ted? Can you really know, with absolute certainty, that your wife isn't trying?

"It doesn't seem like she's trying to me," he said.

"That's not what I asked you. I asked if you can know for sure that she isn't trying. Can you really know if another person is trying or not? What if I told you I didn't think you were trying to save this marriage? Wouldn't you say, 'How would you know if I'm trying, Randy? You have no idea what's going on with me.'"

He relaxed after my question and sighed. "Well, I suppose I can't know if she's trying, but . . ."

"No buts, Ted—a simple yes or no. And you just said, 'No, I can't really know if Jolene is trying.' So now let me ask this. When you think she isn't trying, how do you react? How does that thought affect you?"

"It makes me angry, and I go back and forth between trying harder and giving up. That's where I was before we met you a couple weeks ago. I had just given up trying."

"Let's focus on this one idea, Ted, and I think we'll get to the heart of a lot of your stressful feelings. Take the thought 'Jolene isn't trying' and turn it around. Turn it back to yourself or to the opposite. Do you see what I'm suggesting?" I stood up to my whiteboard and wrote the words "Jolene isn't trying" on the board. "Now take that thought, which you have believed for a while was true, and turn it around. What are some other thoughts you can turn that around to?

"I suppose one thought is 'Jolene is trying.' That would be the opposite, I think."

"Yes, that's perfect. Keep in mind—we're looking for what's true, since believing something false makes us suffer. For that thought 'Jolene really is trying,' ask yourself, is that true? Is it possible that Jolene is trying as best she can to make this marriage work? Is that possibly just as true as your original thought, 'Jolene isn't trying'?"

He thought about what I was asking as he looked at the board. Finally he said, "I suppose it's possible. Maybe she's trying, and I just don't see it."

"Yes," I replied. "She's trying in her own best way, and so are you. Now look for another turnaround for Jolene isn't trying. Turn it back to you this time."

"I'm not trying?" he said, somewhat puzzled. "That can't be true!" I think he felt he had beat the system with this conclusion, but I had other plans.

"A few minutes ago you told me that when Jolene refuses to do what you want, you give up and stop trying. So earlier you blamed Jolene for not trying. But now you admit that at times you have stopped trying and feel like giving up." I gestured to the whiteboard where I had written "Jolene has stopped trying." Then I asked, "Is it just as true that you're not trying, that you have given up on this relationship?"

He looked at me more intently than he had thus far. Clearly he was thinking down a different track than he had in a long time. Twenty minutes earlier he had made a list of all his wife's faults and had set himself up as a self-righteous coach who could make everything better if she would just do what he required. Now he was thinking about how he had given up on the marriage, the very thing he angrily accused her of only minutes earlier.

"Can you think of a few ways in which you have stopped trying, Ted?" I asked, wanting him to think more deeply on this insight.

He lowered his head in thought. "Well, I don't come home at night until she is in bed. I do that to show her I'm fed up with her stupidity. And I refuse to talk about how she feels because I really don't care how she feels."

"And when she can tell that you don't care how she feels, what's the impact on her?" I asked.

"I suppose she feels like giving up. If she can't tell me how she feels, then why try—especially if I've gotten mad at her for trying to explain how she feels." He paused, clearly more reflective and honest now than he had ever been about this important topic.

"Remember what I said when we first began. We're on a search for truth. As we've sorted through your thoughts, we've learned some interesting things. First, we've learned that your core thought 'Jolene isn't trying' is simply not true. But when you believe it's true, it causes you to either push harder or back away. You can probably now see how pushing harder or backing away affects her. And the truth is the opposite of what you initially believed. You *thought* your problems were all caused by Jolene because she wouldn't try and had given up on you and this marriage. The truth, however, is that you have given up and you won't try anymore, which makes it very difficult for your wife when she sees what you are doing and how you treat her. Can you see why uncovering the real truth is so critical in these kinds of situations?"

"Yes," Ted admitted with more sincere humility than I had seen in him thus far.

"So now, armed with the truth, you are able to reclaim the peace your own thoughts drove out of this marriage. Go home, sit down with your wife, and tell her the truth you discovered today. Tell her how you judged her and blamed her. Then tell her the reason for all your marriage problems. Tell her how you actually thought you were doing nothing wrong. Tell her how you had been duped into believing something that was clearly untrue. Apologize for judging and blaming her, and for how you caused her to feel when she was accused by her own husband. That's how you can set right what has been broken, Ted. You now see the real truth of this situation, so go home and make it right. Clean up the mess you have made by believing your negative thoughts."

Ted went home and did as I suggested. The next week we met for counseling, and I found before me two people totally transformed. They still needed direction to rebuild their trust and love, but the truth had set both of them free from the prison of pride and selfishness that thirty years of lies had erected around them. Now, thirty years after this memorable experience, I use a far more elegant and effective process for inquiring into our thoughts than I used back then. No single book has been as useful to me in recent years as *Loving What Is* by Byron Katie. It should be required reading for everyone born into mortality once they get past Dr. Suess and other classics.

CREATING YOUR OWN TURNAROUNDS

This chapter is founded on an important rule of thumb: "Don't believe everything you think." Stressful feelings almost always flow directly from thoughts that we believe are true but that, upon closer examination, we discover are actually false. Believing any thought that is untrue, even if we're unaware of it, generates internal turmoil. In fact, as I've said before, stressful, negative feelings play an important signaling role for us. They alert us of something twisted or erroneous in our thinking. One way to uncover the truth is to first expose the lie. These are not premeditated lies, but they are lies nonetheless. Whenever I believe something that is not true, then I believe a falsehood, a lie. This is mental process that offends the Spirit, causing me to feel internal tension. It is the head trying to take the heart down a painful path and the heart's efforts to resist. By getting our mental deceptions out of our heads and onto paper where they can be examined, the truth is easily visible but not necessarily accepted. In most of us, the determination to be right "at all costs" is strong. After we have been telling a story a certain way for a long time, it has a strong grip on us, and a part of us resists letting it go. What we really resist is taking responsibility, which we tend to equate with blame. No one wants to be blamed.

Here is a simple process you can use to help uncover falsehoods you may currently believe that are holding you back and interfering with your peace and your relationships.

1. Judge another: Even though we've been told not to judge, we do it all the time; we just don't know it. As long as we are controlled by our thoughts and never examine them, they can easily lead us down devilish paths—as Ted learned so well. Think of someone with whom you have strong negative and stressful feelings. Answer the questions Ted answered about your difficult relationship. What do they do that upsets you? What do you think of them? What should they do to help you become happy? What advice would you give them if they would listen?

2. Look at what you have written and ask yourself a few simple questions. For each thought simply look for the lie beneath the thought. Ask, is this true? Can I know it's true for certain? This is a simple yes or no, not a deep analysis of all the possible sides of the question. Look for a thought that you actually cannot verify, even though it feels true. That doesn't count. Of course it feels true. Whatever we think is true, we will also believe.

3. Look for the effects of believing this thought. What impact

does it have on you and on others? How do you treat others when you believe this negative thought about them? How do you treat yourself? In other words, what kind of a person do you become when you hold onto this stressful thought? Are you angry, childish, irritated, judgmental, or something else?

4. Like Ted, take the thoughts you have about others and turn them back to yourself. Remember what really disturbs us—our thoughts about others and external circumstances, not those external people and things. If your thought is "He should be more caring, kinder, and less critical," turn it around to yourself. "I should be more kind, more concerned, and less critical." Then look for times in your interaction when you have been unkind or critical. Apply the judgment of another to yourself. Try to find examples when you have said, done, or thought in ways that make the turned around statement just as true as your judgment of the other person. See if you can find in yourself what you blame and accuse others of having done. Remember, this is not about blame. It is simply an effort to find the truth amid a host of lies you have bought into, even though you didn't know it. You are asking one basic but critical question. "Is it possible that I possess the same negative qualities that I judge them for having?" Whatever you accuse them of, find that same tendency in yourself. This not only increases your compassion but places the focus where it must belong in order for you to find the freedom you seek. It is really an escape from the darkness of the flawed thoughts you believe are true. This can be a powerful discovery if we are willing and ready to change.

Notes
1. Epictetus, http://en.wikipedia.org/wiki/Epictetus.

YOU GET TO SAY

I first met Pete in a class I was teaching at a local business school. That semester I had around ninety students. Pete certainly didn't stand out as anything special. Many participated more than Pete, did better on exams, and put together more impressive presentations. Until I learned otherwise, I thought Pete was a fairly average student, with no extraordinary abilities.

Near the end of the semester, I heard about a contest in the business school that all students were invited to enter. Students were asked to form a virtual company with two or three others students. They were to develop a business and marketing plan, define a product or service, and project the financials for their new start-up. The contest would be judged by representatives from actual venture capital companies connected with the universities. The winning students would be awarded $200,000 toward launching their business and receive hands-on coaching from one of the venture capital firms.

The weeks passed, and I thought no more about the contest. One day there was an air of excitement in the classroom as the students entered. I asked what all the buzz was about. "Today they announce the winner of the big venture capital contest," said one of the students with obvious enthusiasm "We all think Pete's team will win the big money."

"You mean our Pete?" I asked a bit surprised, "The Pete in this class?"

"Yes," cried several students at once. "Pete's going to be rich and famous. One day you can tell everyone that you were his teacher!" This brought a roar of laughter around the room. Sure enough, later that day the winner was announced, and as predicted, Pete and his team won the $200,000.

Two weeks later the semester ended, and I never saw Pete again. Then one day, nearly a year later, I ran into Pete at the gym where I work out. He and his friends had actually launched two different businesses, both going fairly well, but they needed more capital to grow to the next level.

"We've got a presentation to a venture capital firm in San Francisco next week," Pete explained. "If that goes well, we will have the money we need to move our business forward." He was understandably excited about the possibilities and promised to keep me in the loop on how things turned out. As we parted, I thought how different Pete was from me when I was in my early twenties. He talked about meeting with big-shots from San Francisco with no apparent apprehension whatsoever. I could have never done that. Even if the opportunity would have presented itself, I didn't have the self-confidence to even attempt it. My fear of failure would have kept me from even trying.

Two weeks later, I saw Pete again and was eager to learn how his big presentation had gone.

"We made our presentation, like I told you, and they turned us down," he said. I began to console him for failing and tell him how disappointing it must be when he interrupted.

"No, it was great." He grinned. "After they rejected our proposal, we asked them what we could have done better. It was fantastic. They told us exactly what we need to do next time to get their support. So even though we didn't get the money, we know exactly what to do at our next meeting. It was perfect, and I learned a ton. I'm excited to meet with them again next month." As he walked away, I realized I had misjudged Pete. I had thought he was a pretty ordinary young man. But I had just learned that he had some extraordinary traits that few people possess so naturally. That day Pete taught me a tremendous lesson, and I now realize why he and his team won the contest. He may not have been the smartest student in the program and certainly didn't have anywhere near the highest GPA. But what he did have, in such natural abundance that he didn't even realize it, was incredible optimism. Of the various negative ways he could have interpreted the unsuccessful presentation, he drew the one conclusion that very few would. He didn't blame himself or his team. He wasn't frustrated by the outcome nor did he interpret the experience in any negative way. He firmly believed that there was no such thing as failure, only more information about how to succeed.

He and his colleagues went into that meeting needing capital for their business and walked out empty-handed. Most people would judge that as a failure, a setback, or a reason to second-guess the viability of the business. After all, a group of bright, successful, and wealthy investors had reviewed their business plan and decided not to invest in its future. This must mean that these experienced people knew something that the three new college graduates didn't. As far as I could tell, none of this deterred Pete from his long-term goal. When Pete heard the words "We're not supporting this project," he translated that decision into useful feedback and asked, "What could we have done differently that would have worked better? What can we do next time that will increase the odds of success?" He used a setback as a learning experience. And in so doing, he avoided all the feelings that a negative interpretation would have caused, such as disappointment, dejection, and uncertainty about the future. In addition, Pete and his team walked away with critical information about what to do better next time.

Pete didn't win that contest because he was naturally brilliant, a polished speaker, or the top student in the business school. He won because of how he explained setbacks, negative surprises, and disappointment. He didn't believe in them. He had a way of explaining setbacks in positive, productive ways. His mind-set was grounded in optimistic thinking. He explained seeming setbacks in temporary ways that enabled him to move past them with relative ease, avoiding the stress and negativity that most people create by explaining setbacks in pessimistic ways.

Like Pete, we all explain and interpret life's setbacks and negative surprises when they occur. This is how the mind works. A part of our mind is dedicated to solving problems. A setback or negative surprise—a sore trial, if you will—is viewed as a problem. When such things occur, the mind leaps into gear to solve the problems. It tries to explain and then dissect them, and we interpret what has happened, why, and what it means. Sometimes the mind follows a pessimistic line of thought that generates a host of negative, stressful feelings. And sometimes, as with Pete, it explains a setback in an optimistic way, thereby avoiding the emotional turmoil and agitation that so often afflict us.

Here's how this chain of events plays out. Initially we have what appears to be a negative experience and we *make it mean* something. At the speed of thought, the mind decides what the experience means, provides explanations for why things occurred as they did, and even projects how the future will be as a result of this experience. Some have called the mind a "meaning making machine," and in many ways that's exactly what is. With no effort or conscious involvement from us, it spins away, night and day, interpreting, offering opinions, judging what an experience means, and even warning us of the uncertain future.

We learned earlier that by themselves, our experiences are neither positive nor negative. Events in and of themselves are meaning*less* until we make them meaning*ful* by how we explain them. Consider the following list of events and decide, if you can, if they are positive or negative.

- You are diagnosed with cancer at an early age.
- A tragic accident at work leaves you paralyzed from the waist down and wheelchair-bound for the rest of your life.
- Your company was just purchased by Microsoft. Your stock options make you an overnight millionaire.
- You are offered a job that pays twice the money you are currently earning but requires you to be gone 50 percent of the time from your spouse and four young children at home.
- After twenty years of marriage, most of it unhappy, your spouse files for divorce.
- After twenty years of being happily married, your spouse has an affair and is excommunicated.

Anyone who has an experience like one of these goes through an automatic mental process in which he interprets what this experience means, who's to blame, why it happened, and what it will mean for the future. The mistake is not just in making our experiences mean something negative and stressful but in never questioning the accuracy of our interpretations. What we fail to see is the power we have over our circumstances and our interpretations. Our power lies in our ability to explain our setbacks however we choose. The events are meaningless. They are merely events, things that happen every day. But once they occur, we alone decide what they mean, and we do it unconsciously and automatically, all the time.

When we interpret a setback, we tap into a dimension of agency of which we are largely unaware. We tend to think of agency in very broad and superficial terms—choosing good over evil, right from wrong, making a righteous decision rather than the opposite. But most of us don't make these kinds of choices on a regular basis. What we do choose several times a day is how to interpret what our experiences mean. We are constantly making meaning out of our everyday experiences even when we have no idea we're doing it. God has given us the power to choose our response to whatever happens to us. For any given experience, there are countless ways we can respond—some of them helpful and productive, some which bring upon us all manner of unnecessary emotional burdens. Many times these emotional burdens could have been avoided with a different explanation. Thus what we make things mean determines, to a large degree, the feelings we have and the very quality of our day to day lives.

Take my friend Pete, for example. He prepared for weeks to meet with a group of heavy hitters from San Francisco, many twice his age. He and his team did everything they could to ensure success, and a lot was riding on how the investors would react. Pete and his team made their presentation and after some discussion, the investors said, "No thanks, we think we'll pass." That little string of words, "No thanks, we'll pass" in fact, means *nothing*. Pete didn't have their money when he walked in and didn't have it when he walked out, so no harm was done. How Pete explains those words to himself and how he and his team feels and reacts after the meeting is completely up to Pete and his team. They can make the experience mean anything they want. This meeting could be the straw that breaks the camel's back, and the business could subsequently dissolve as Pete and his teammates all go their separate ways or the meeting could be a catalyst for more aggressive growth of the business in the future. But the situation doesn't determine what it means, Pete and his friends make that decision.

This insight is much more than a superficial pop-psychology pump up maxim. It reflects a deeper understanding of the power we each have to create the kinds of lives we live. Life does have its ups and downs as we know so well. But we get to decide what they mean and how they will affect us. How we explain our experiences sets the stage for so much that happens later on. When I decide that losing a job is a terrible tragedy from which I will not soon recover, this pessimistic, negative stream of thought sets me up for further failure and additional emotional suffering. The seemingly simple act of explaining an event in a different way sets into motion a different chain of events, different feelings, and vastly different reactions. How we respond to one trial, setback, or surprise forecasts all that follows, at least until we learn to see things differently and invent a different explanation. It all rests firmly in our hands.

This is a book about making sense of our setbacks, difficulties, and negative surprises. Our goal is to learn ways to respond to our experiences in productively and prevent as much unnecessary emotional suffering as possible. In most cases, we generate our negative, stressful feelings by how we explain our challenging experiences. Time and time again, studies reveal that a pessimistic interpretation of a life event has a significant emotional impact. It leaves us feeling hopeless and helpless, which increases our despair and discouragement. We're not discouraged by what took place but by our interpretations of that event. Such negative interpretations also make it harder to move past difficult experiences. Even very good people can struggle endlessly over a difficult experience when their struggles arise from their interpretation of what occurred and why.

A dear friend recently lost his wife to a sudden heart attack. She was only fifty-three and had no history of heart problems. This painful, negative experience would bring most people to their knees. But what did he make it mean? How did he explain it to himself? And who gets to decided what it means if not him? Because of the suddenness of her passing, he decided that God had taken her, which sent him into even deeper questions about why God would do such a thing. Why would God take his wife in the prime of her life? All they had planned to do together—travel, missions, and enjoying their grandchildren—had now been destroyed by this experience. Eventually, this good man's faith began to slacken as he grew bitter over God taking his wife and bringing upon him so many trials and heavy emotional burdens. Friends and family knew that he had not been the same since losing his wife but were puzzled over his church inactivity. Then he revealed what he had made this experience mean, and the rest of the story made complete sense. He could have explained it in a dozen different ways, some useful and some very stressful and counterproductive. When we explain what a setback means and why it took place, we draw upon our agency. But far too often we create a negative, stressful, pessimistic interpretation that generates burdensome emotions and drains us of hope and faith. A different explanation would have led to different feelings and different spiritual outcomes.

After thirty years of research on optimism and pessimism, Dr. Martin Seligman wrote, "Your way of explaining events to yourself determines how helpless you become. We all have a style of explaining bad events to ourselves. These habits of thought began in childhood and become more permanent during adolescence."[1] His research transformed the field of psychology from a focus on mysterious psychological defects to analyzing how people think when they fail. Not surprisingly, people who adopt a pessimistic explanatory style get depressed much more easily than those who think about things in optimistic ways, even when they face identical events.

Your habits of thought have been with you for a very long time. They are knee-jerk reflexive reactions to your experiences. Pete didn't just "put on a happy face" when things failed to turn out as he hoped. He wasn't "smiling through his tears," as some people try unsuccessfully to do. His optimistic reaction reflected a fundamental habit of thought—a way of viewing all life experiences, including those we might typically label as negative. Your response reveals your personal habits of thought that you learned in childhood and that have been deeply rooted since then. Your "explanatory style" reflects your beliefs about what causes your setbacks and negative surprises.

For example, suppose you are doing all you can to find a new job and nothing turns up. Prayer, effort, and networking has led nowhere. Your mind labels this as a problem and when you face a problem, your mind wants to solve it, explain it, and analyze it. But the way you explain it, the cause you ascribe to your difficulties, is significant. Think of the myriad explanations you could invent for this one simple little challenge.

+ I'm just not good enough for the kinds of jobs that are out there right now.
+ This kind of thing always happens to me. I should just stay where I am, even though my current job makes me miserable.
+ Looks like God doesn't want me to work right now. Guess I'll stay home for a while.
+ Looks like I can't find work with someone else, so maybe there's

some kind of company I can start on my own. I think I'll look into it.

We could list dozens of possible ways to explain the reason for not finding a job. So which one is right? Which is the *correct* explanation for why things aren't working out? Obviously this is the wrong question. Since each explanation will dictate how you feel, what you will do next, and how hopeful you will be about the future, you should choose the explanation that will result in the least amount of stress and negativity in your life. The right question to ask is, "Which explanation will serve me best?"

You alone get to decide what your experiences mean. You alone explain why your circumstances are not what you would like them to be. You alone have the power to make the events in your life mean anything you'd like them to mean. But be careful. The way you explain the cause of an unwelcome event sets you up for either productive or unproductive actions thereafter.

How we *feel* depends on how we *think*. This means that how we explain the causes for setbacks and trials determines the impact those experiences will have on us and the strength and duration of the emotions that accompany them. Thus the same experience explained in two different ways will lead to two very different ends and vastly different emotions.

While there are clearly gradations, let's discuss two primary explanatory styles: optimistic and pessimistic. These are as different as can be. Pessimistic people explain setbacks in personal, permanent, and pervasive ways. In other words, they tell themselves, "It's me—my faults, my weaknesses, my shortcomings, my imperfections," and "This setback will last a long time and affect all areas of my life." It's not surprising that when we think about setbacks in these kinds of ways we become depressed and have a much harder time bouncing back. Pessimists also tend to ruminate over their setbacks. They can't let anything go. They think about their experiences endlessly—sometimes for months or even years. They're always talking about their problems to friends, colleagues, and church leaders. They simply cannot get over the fact that they failed or that things have failed to turn out as they hoped. But, of course, if a person blames himself for the negative experiences in his life and honestly believes the effects will last forever and spill into every avenue of his existence, it's little wonder he's bound down with burdensome emotions.

But let's keep in mind that people are not either pessimists or optimists as they are male or female. We're referring to explanatory styles, the way people think about setbacks and negative surprises, not to the people themselves. Each individual person is a son or daughter of God with divine potential. However, each has developed habits of thought, some of which many not serve him well, making difficult experiences far worse than they need to be.

Optimistic people have the same kinds of difficult experiences but think about them in different ways. Pete is a perfect example of how optimists explain seemingly bad events. He did not take his rejection personally, which pessimists almost always do. Instead he told himself, "We didn't have all the necessary information. Next time we'll have everything they need to see to make a positive decision." He viewed his setback as temporary not permanent. "They said no, but we asked what we could do better and we're going back better prepared." All Pete did was make this experience mean something very different from what a less optimistic person might.

Pessimists tend to catastrophize negative events, turning a single experience into a major trial. Habits of thought, pessimistic or optimistic, are deeply rooted in our thoughts and tend to arise automatically. People who catastrophize tend to do it regardless of the issue. It reflects their habitual, automatic way of responding to the slightest setback or surprise. Pessimistic thinking leads people to believe a negative experience will affect them in pervasive ways, coloring every aspect of their lives. Optimists are better at compartmentalizing negative events. Pete failed to get the capital he needed, but this had nothing to do with his dating life, exercise habits, church attendance, and so on, so Pete did not allow those things to be affected by his setback. For optimists there is little spill-over into other aspects of their lives, but for ardent pessimists, there nearly always is.

I once had a conversation with a woman who had a dreary pessimistic view of her difficulties. She worked for a tough boss and had recently had her performance review. She'd received a lower rating than she was expecting, which would affect her pay rate for the following year. That was the event. How she thought about it turned her inside out with worry, fear, and anxiety over the future. "Now I can't quit work as I was planning. I can't afford it. And I was going back to school and now that can't happen, and if I don't go now, I'll never go, and if I never go, then I'll be stuck in this rotten job for the rest of my life, and then . . . ." You get the picture. I watched her stress level increase drastically in the ten minutes we chatted about this one experience. Because of her pessimistic explanation for this small setback, she was bringing upon herself all kinds of unnecessary emotional suffering. As I spoke with her, I could foresee all that would happen in the following weeks. She would likely need a priesthood blessing and several meetings with her bishop to calm her down and ease her worries. Her home teachers would be called several times during the next month as she became so worried that she couldn't sleep or fulfill her church calling. This one event—thought about and ruminated on in a pessimistic way—would produce a mountain of fear and deep emotional pain. Such is the astonishing power of the mind and the interpretations we give to our experiences.

LEARNING OPTIMISM

One curious fact that we have already established several times in this volume is that whatever thoughts rise up in our minds, we believe they are true, even if we have no evidence of their truth. Rarely do we have a negative thought and pause long enough to examine it for truth. If we think it, then it must be true—or so we presume. This fuzzy logic grows even more distorted when our emotions get involved. We use our emotions as proof that what we believe really is valid and true. We reason that if it wasn't true, we wouldn't feel this way. In fact, our negative feelings confirm nothing except that stressful thoughts and stories are running around in our heads. Stressful thoughts, when accepted as true, will always generate stressful and negative emotions. If I think I'm stupid, I'll feel bad and sad. If I think I have potential to succeed, regardless of setbacks, I'll press forward in the face of seeming failure. I'll keep trying and I'll persist when others may give up. My feelings of confidence and determination will spring from my belief that I can succeed if I work hard and keep trying. If I embrace a thought such as *I've never been good at test taking so I'll never do well in classes that have a lot of tests*, then a different string of feelings will follow.

Our thinking sets up our feelings. Our negative feelings essentially indicate that we are embracing and believing negative thoughts, which is why we feel as we do. Except in rare cases of chemical or hormonal imbalances, which can wreak havoc on our moods, our feelings flow directly and automatically from the way we think about and explain our difficulties. A pessimistic explanation sets into motion a completely different feeling than an optimistic explanation for the same event. Thus how we explain life's difficult events is key to our understanding them.

Research has also demonstrated that we are not born pessimistic or optimistic. These are learned habits of thought that often begin in childhood and then are confirmed in adolescence. Children observe how their parents and other adults react to various life experiences and from these examples, they learn how to respond. When curious children ask why something bad happened they might just as well be asking, "What does this mean? How am I to make sense of difficult experiences? How am I supposed to react when difficult setbacks and negative surprises happen?" They have no idea how to respond to such experiences until they learn from others. Perhaps no more life lesson is more important than when parents teach, by word and actions, how to respond to trials and stern setbacks.

Positive and negative examples abound of how a parent's reaction to trying circumstances affects his child. One couple looked forward to the birth of their first granddaughter. But during delivery, serious complications ensued and both mother and baby died. Their heartbreak and shock soon turned into bitterness and blame. They filed a lawsuit against the hospital and doctor for malpractice and negligence. Attorneys, doing what attorneys do, stirred this couple and their other children into an angry frenzy. Soon their bitterness turned to revenge. They would not only sue for damages and retribution for their losses, they would destroy the reputation of the unqualified doctor. As is often the case, their bitterness and blame spread to God. They questioned why He had permitted this tragedy, why He had not intervened. It wasn't long before their church activity ceased and they rejected every attempt by concerned neighbors and friends to comfort them. They didn't even want comfort. They wanted revenge.

What these parents failed to consider was the message they were sending to their children about how to respond to life's difficulties. From this experience their children learned that when tragedy strikes, God has let you down and failed to keep His promises. "Is that the kind of God we worship?" cried the heart-broken father. "If so, I want nothing to do with Him or anyone who believes in such an uncaring God." The conversations about their tragedy that likely occurred around this family's dinner table cemented in the children's minds how to react when things fail to turn out as you want. The message they received was, "You don't turn to God; you blame Him. You don't strive for greater faith; you try to get even with those who have wronged you. You don't give thanks for your blessings; you reject God for not blessing you as you wanted." The message was clear and was easily received by the children. You can imagine the spiritual fallout from this experience. Two generations later, faith is frail and dozens of family members have rejected God and religion altogether.

Conversely I know of two other families who have lost two grandchildren in one year. Not long ago, members of both families stood in testimony meeting and publicly gave thanks for the love and support shown them through their trials. "While this has been a sad and difficult time for our family," said one wife, "we have had some very powerful spiritual experiences that have brought our family much closer than we ever were before." Their examples of faith and trust in God, notwithstanding their deep trials, inspire all who know them. They have provided their children and grandchildren with a clear spiritual blueprint for how to respond in productive ways to the trials and setbacks of life.

We parents must understand that we are constantly sending messages to our children by what we say, how we say it, and how we behave, especially when taxing trials or even minor setbacks occur. A father whose temper easily flares when things don't go his way teaches his children to respond with anger when they don't get what they want. A drive down the highway reveals to his children what to say and do when other drivers are "idiots." Children imitate our words, and in time, they emulate our actions for good or ill. We show them how to respond. We teach them what things mean, we provide vivid examples of how to explain setbacks and negative surprises. Thus we either set them upon a path that can bless their lives when trials come, as they surely will, or we harm them by our own rash and sometimes counterproductive behavior.

We must be careful and cautious when teaching these important lessons. These are certainly some of the most important lessons our children will ever learn. As parents we have two primary questions when facing our own trials. First, what will I make this mean for myself? And second, what message will my response teach my children? A third implied question is this: what would the Lord have me teach in order to best prepare my children to face the vicissitudes of life that they will undoubtedly face in the future?

"Don't cry over spilt milk"—one of Grandma's favorite sayings—is still good advice. When children see our strong overreactions to daily setbacks, like spilt milk, they learn to exaggerate small, insignificant events into minor emotional breakdowns. These children are then ill-prepared for the ups and downs of life. Conversely, when we show our children by our actions and words that little things really are little, we teach crucial life lessons. Our actions say, "That's no big deal, honey—accidents happen." Children learn crucial life lessons from us, their parents, that they can learn nowhere else in such a consistent way.

Tips for Unlearning Pessimism

While reading this chapter you may have realized, much to your dismay, that you tend to view life through pessimistic lenses. You may have a tendency to "catastrophize," turning small setbacks into major emotional meltdowns. Since such habits of thought were *learned*, they can also be unlearned. True, it takes conscious effort and awareness, but it can be done. Here are some suggestions:

1. **Notice:** The hardest part about unlearning is first noticing when you leap off with your pessimistic bungee cords, not having any idea what you're doing or what the consequences will be. Keep in mind that your habits of thought arise automatically and immediately and that they are very familiar. Since this is the way you have always thought and reacted to difficult experiences, large and small, you will not notice your habits of thought unless you make a deliberate effort to do so. One way to do this is by keeping a journal of your thoughts and reactions. Record the events that happen throughout the day and your thoughts about or reactions to those events. Do this for a day or two and then review your list, looking for patterns. You should notice some of the habits of thought that limit your peace, undermine your joy, and generate stressful, troublesome feelings. Our tendency is to think of the event, person, or experience as causing these feelings. That's untrue. Your stressful feelings flow directly and automatically from

the way you think about what has happened, from what you make it mean.

2. **See the puzzle:** When setbacks or negative surprises occur, we are often awash with conflicting thoughts, feelings, and questions. These are all part of a pattern or puzzle that can be fitted together. In other words, you will see, if you begin to fit the pieces together, that first something occurs—a phone call, an email, a conversation with a friend or family member. We call this an event. Such events are not stressful, hard, or depressing. They are simply events that in fact mean nothing until we make them mean something. Notice what you make them mean, as suggested earlier, and then see the pattern of feelings and additional snowballing thoughts that follow your interpretation. One stressful thought usually prods others that increase in intensity and emotional power. Catch this cycle early, and you can avoid unnecessary emotional suffering. Begin to see the chain of events from initial experience to your thoughts about that event, to your feelings, to additional stressful thoughts and feelings, and so on.

3. **Explain things differently:** Reframing is simply thinking about a situation, person, or event differently. Countless reactions are possible for any event. Perhaps you tend to select the most stressful one available, which is how you generate a pile of stress in your life. But this can all be avoided when you learn to substitute automatic pessimistic thoughts with more optimistic ones. This is far more than putting a smile on your face when you feel terribly sad inside. This reframing process involves reclaiming your power over your feelings by changing how you make sense of your experiences. The only reason you feel as you do lies in how you interpret your experiences. Change the thought, make a different interpretation, draw a different conclusion, and your feelings will follow like an obedient puppy. Your feelings take direction from your thoughts, judgments, and interpretations, from what you make things mean, how you explain your experiences. As you learn to respond to your experiences with more positive interpretations, you will change your world in profound ways, all by simply changing your mind.

Notes

1. Christopher Peterson, Steven F. Maier, and Martin E. P. Seligman, *Learned Helplessness: A Theory for the Age of Personal Control* (New York: Oxford University Press, 1995).

THE END OF
SUFFERING

As the huge gong rang, signaling that it was time to begin, everyone who'd been chatting in the hallways filed into the inviting meeting room. Large windows overlooked the majestic Caribbean. These people had gathered from all around the world for a mindfulness seminar. Most had no idea what mindfulness even was, much less how to become more mindful. They were about to learn.

On the table before each person was a simple white napkin and on it, three raisins. After everyone was settled, the teacher began.

"We'll begin with a small snack. But before you eat, I have a few ground rules. First, pick up only one of the raisins but don't eat it. I want you to look at this raisin. Really notice it. Roll it around in your fingers if you like. Notice its texture, size, and overall shape. If you like, you can compare its shape, size, and texture to the other two raisins we've provided for your snack. Take a moment or two and really look at these little pieces of food carefully. You've probably eaten thousands of these little things over your lifetime but never really noticed them or paid much attention. This time, I'm asking you to pay attention to what you normally overlook."

As people began to carefully examine the raisins, several whispered comments. "Interesting," one man said to himself, lost in the exercise.

Others simply said, "Hmm," as if they had never really seen a raisin before.

After several minutes of examining the raisins, the teacher continued, "Now I want you to take one of these raisins and put it in your mouth, but before you do, let me guide you. Notice your arm reaching for the raisin. Notice the movement of your hand, fingers, and thumb as it grasps this little raisin. Pay attention to the movement from the table to your mouth. Before putting it in your mouth, raise it to your nose and smell it, taking in all the subtle aromas of this little raisin. Then slowly put the raisin in your mouth but do not chew yet. Feel the raisin with your tongue. Roll it around in your mouth a bit to get a fuller sense of its shape, size, and subtle taste. Note any thoughts about liking or disliking raisins. When you're ready, bite the raisin, and as you do, pay attention to your teeth mashing the raisin and to the swallowing motion that follows. Try to notice how it feels after you swallow as the raisin bits and saliva move down your throat to your stomach. Notice as many parts of this fascinating process as you can."

The teacher sat down while everyone in the room followed his instructions. A few people giggled as they did something so slowly that they would normally have done in mere seconds. One woman commented, "If I was at the movies I would have had an entire box eaten by now!" Everyone chuckled in recognition that she was absolutely right. When it looked like everyone was through eating their snack, the teacher once more stood up and asked, "What did you notice as you did this exercise?"

Several people began talking at once, excited to share what they had noticed from eating a raisin differently than they would have normally done.

"I realize that I never notice these kinds of things," admitted a nurse from a local hospital. "It makes me wonder how many other things I do on autopilot, even in my work with patients. I might be missing a lot of very important things happening all around me."

Someone else added, "It makes me wonder if I have any idea what goes in my mouth. No wonder I'm fifty pounds overweight. Usually when I eat, I'm completely oblivious to what I'm eating, how it tastes, or how I feel while eating. That's eye-opening. I enjoyed eating one raisin much more than I usually enjoy an entire bag of raisins at home. Interesting."

"When I am totally unaware of what I'm doing," observed another, "like I would have been before this exercise, it's like I'm out of control, kind of like my body and mind are on autopilot and I'm off somewhere else, clueless to what I'm actually doing. Eating even little things like raisins make me wonder how many other much more important things I do out of robotic habit."

These people were learning to be more mindful of everyday experiences, so easily taken for granted. "Knowing what you are doing when you are doing it is the essence of mindfulness," declared Dr. Jon Kabat-Zinn, who first developed this simple raisin exercise. "All mindfulness involves is paying attention to your experience from moment to moment. This leads directly to new ways of seeing and being in your life."[1]

Every chapter in this book has been an invitation to become more mindful, more aware of your life experience, of your thoughts about that experience and what you make it all mean. You learned that you have a voice in your head, constantly chattering away. Learning to be more mindful of this voice is crucial to your ongoing peace and joy. Lack of awareness is the equivalent to being dragged along by a rushing river of thought, oblivious to what is happening and why. At such times you are not only unaware but unable to act with wisdom, so caught up in the stressful content of your thinking. Also, lack of awareness always creates suffering of some kind, because the mind's natural and most automatic state is "carnal, sensual, and devilish" (Moses 5:13). When Adam and Eve fell, they experienced a change in their way of thinking. Prior to the Fall, their desires were simple and pure, like a child's. But after the Fall, their fallen minds and their compulsive habits of thought led them, and the rest of us, to think in highly self-defeating and counterproductive ways. Hence we are commanded to put off the natural man, for this kind of thinking and reasoning makes us an enemy to God (see Mosiah 3:19). It leads us to think, feel, and behave in ways that separate us from spiritual things and the peace that comes from the presence of the Spirit.

While the scriptures say that "the natural man is an enemy to God," a more accurate description is that the natural way we think, our most automatic habits of thought, are at times devilish indeed (Mosiah 3:19). But this dark veil is not impenetrable. Stressful thoughts, spun by the natural mind, only have power over us when we are unaware, when we lack mindfulness. This lack of awareness makes it easy to be caught up in our stressful thoughts, which leads to all kinds of negative outcomes. In a sense, the only reason we suffer from trials, setbacks, and surprises is that we are unaware of our mind and its tendency to make everything a problem. If we are fully caught up in our thoughts, especially in times of stress, we are easily overcome by our mind's relentless current. Thus it is absolutely essential to see that you are not your thoughts. Your mind spins on without your involvement or approval. You have no control over it. If you did, you would tell it what to do, when to stop thinking, and when to shut up in the middle of the night when you can't sleep.

If you were actually your thoughts, you would dictate the kinds of thoughts on which you wanted to reflect. You would issue a command: "Today I will not worry over past regrets and dreams unrealized. That's pointless. Nor will I worry over the uncertain future, which is equally pointless. I will live fully in the moment and not allow old patterns of thought rob me of my peace and joy."

But you and I can't do this. As we slip into bed at night, we often discover, to our utter irritation, that our minds are awash with chaotic and relentless thoughts we can do nothing about. If we were really in charge of our thoughts, we would simply shut them off and go to sleep. That's why we say that our minds seem to have minds of their own. And they run on different instructions than we would give, working off their own agendas, at times fully opposite from what we genuinely want. Learning that we are not our minds nor our thoughts is the beginning of freedom—the profound realization that you and the thoughts constantly being spun out inside your head are not the same. It's as if deep inside our brains there is a little mechanism whose only job is to constantly generate thoughts of every conceivable kind. These thoughts appear inside our head as if out of nowhere. We don't consciously think them. They simply appear. And we realize, when we pay attention, that we can do nothing to stop this incessant and involuntary mechanism from doing its job. Day and night, week after week, year after year, this tiny thought generator churns away, filling our heads with what seems like an inner dialogue or running commentary on everything.

Much of what appears in our heads or what we hear as the voices in our heads is harmless, and some of it is useful and serves us well. But consciously using our minds is different from our minds using us. How can our minds use us? This happens whenever they generate stressful, negative thoughts and we believe these thoughts are true. A thought appears and we believe it because it's inside our heads. Matching emotions and actions follow, consistent with what we think is true. And when this chain of events happens without our slightest awareness, we might say that our minds are using us, our stressful thoughts are running the show, and we have lost control. This is the sad root of all of the emotional pain that afflicts us and causes us to suffer.

I was recently asked to reduce everything in this book down to one idea that would enable people to make real changes in their lives. "Learning to be more mindful is the key," I said with no hesitation. "All of the difficulties discussed in this volume arise because we are not mindful, lack awareness, and are cut off from sources of truth and wisdom. This happens because we are completely caught up in the frenzied, chaotic content of our minds."

It is so easy to get swallowed up by the thick of thin things. We can walk through a park and barely notice the symphony of sound all around us. The birds, the gentle breeze, the nearby rushing of water over rock, the distant sound of children at play. And where are we at such times? What prevents us from noticing? The answer: We are swallowed up in the content of our own thoughts, miles away in our mind, thinking, worrying, ruminating, or spinning stories. We're not present to anything but the constant internal chatter of our minds. And we're not really aware of that either, for in fact we are totally swept away by the content of our minds and don't realize it. We're too busy thinking, ruminating, concentrating, and mulling over this or that to even notice that we're doing these things. We're not naturally mindful. It takes effort and deliberate attention to step back from the current of constant thought and simply be aware, notice, and pay attention to what the mind is doing. But as we make this effort, the onrush of incessant thought begins to slow, and we become more mindful, more aware. Every chapter in this book features people who became so caught up in the content of their stressful minds that they acted in self-defeating ways, which caused them deep emotional pain. The solution to all these challenges is learning to step back from the chatter of the voices in your head and simply notice.

Several years ago I was passing through one of the darkest trials of my life. Never have I felt the effects of a completely stressed out mind as I did at this time. Worry and fear consumed me like never before in my life. Everywhere I went my anxious thoughts and the stressful feelings they produced went with me. Some friends invited me to go camping with them in the nearby mountains, and I took them up on it. *Maybe this will be good for me*, I thought. *Maybe if I can get away from everything for a few days it will be helpful.*

What I didn't realize was just how pesky stressful thoughts can be. They follow you everywhere, even to the tops of mountains. The first morning I arose early and went for a short hike on my own. I sat on a rock, overlooking a beautiful mountain lake and a clear blue sky overhead. The scene was truly stunning. But as I sat there, surrounded by everything peaceful, my worries started up, my fears of the future rushed in, and before I knew it, I had lost control of my mind. I wasn't running my life in a positive direction. My intensely stressful thoughts had taken over, and I had no idea how to stop them. I was literally "swallowed up" by the negative, stressful contents of my mind. Had I been more mindful, I could have devoted myself to greater awareness of what was running through my head and its impact on me. But largely unaware, we are no match for the powerful current of stressful thoughts that often overtake us.

The mind is bound up in time. Under duress, it broods over the past, ruminating on old regrets, dreams unfulfilled, things we should have done or avoided, missed opportunities. We could be sitting on a park bench near the beautiful ocean, surrounded by scenes of peace and tranquility and be totally taken over by sadness, old regrets, and all that might have been. Thus the precious present is clouded by the past as the mind attaches and ruminates on things gone by. We are only anxious in the present because we think endlessly about the past in negative ways. What could be more pointless than regret and sadness over what lies behind us? All the thinking in the world will not change it, and yet such brooding can spill into our present and we lose our awareness of the moment. Thus we speak of mindfulness as a moment to moment awareness, free of brooding over the past or fretting over the uncertain future.

Recently a dear friend of mine was diagnosed with advanced prostate cancer. An experience like this can kick-start the time-bound mind like few things in life. Imagine what might run through his mind unless he is aware enough to observe his thoughts with careful attention and dispel the power they would otherwise exert over him. More than likely he will obsess over all that he might have done or should have done to prevent this diagnosis. He will not only be physically ill but emotionally taxed as well, which certainly won't be helpful. Likely he will spend a lot of time in the future fretting over his wife, children, and the business and finance matters still left undone. It's easy to see that with one word—*cancer*—his mind will shift into high gear in seconds, making an already jarring experience an emotional tsunami. His stress level will shoot up to an all-time high as he thinks and worries and frets and obsesses over the past and the future. Unless he knows how to focus on moment-to-moment awareness, his life will be held hostage from now on by an endless stream of stressful, negative, and fearful thoughts.

This is not a comment about the man himself, his mental soundness, or his personal righteousness. It's merely an illustration of what happens to most of us when facing adversity, setbacks, or harsh negative surprises. Left to run amuck, this is what the time-bound mind does, naturally, unconsciously, and compulsively. Its primary job, if you will, is to make us suffer, to add insult to misery. Remember the mind, or at least part of it, is "carnal, sensual, and devilish" (Moses 5:13). Thus its patterns are reactive and often dysfunctional. They serve no productive purpose.

Intuitively we understand this but usually have no idea how to apply it on a regular basis. We say to such stressed out individuals, "Don't worry, everything will be all right." But such simplistic attempts to encourage others are of little effect against the comparatively strong power of incessant thought. "I try not to worry about it, but I can't stop," these individuals might respond. This feeling of helplessness before the relentless mental chatter is something we can all relate to. It seems to operate independently from you and me. At times it directly opposes what we most desire. When we long for peace and contentment in our stressful lives, we find nothing inside but an endless stream of things to fret over, fear, and ruminate about, as if all of that will somehow diminish the grip our mind has over us.

Think of the great difference between noticing that you are stressed out and anxious and learning to be mindful of how you interpret your experiences. It is one thing to realize that you are swamped with stressful thoughts you can't shut off, but this doesn't quell the fears or decrease the distress you feel. To know that you are worried and full of negative thoughts doesn't give you added power over them. Mindfulness involves stepping back from this rushing river of thought and simply observing it, noticing it, and watching it as a curious bystander. When you are mindful, you will notice the kinds of things that your mind is thinking about, worrying about, and trying to tell you, as if you were the student and it were the experienced teacher. Pay attention to your thoughts, the feelings they invoke, and your reactions to what is happening around you. As you shine the light of awareness on what normally consumes you, it loses its hold on you. Those typically ignored thoughts shrink back in the presence of your awareness. The exercise brings your full presence to something you were oblivious to only moments before. Soon you will see two separate entities. The voice spinning away and you, observing the voice. This recognition that you are not that voice and that therefore you are not inextricably bound up in its content is true liberation.

Many people wonder why they think the way they do. They want to know where the habitual patterns of their stressful thinking originated. It's all an extension of our life experiences, training, education, and cultural conditioning. The way we most naturally think now, especially in the face of life's difficulties, has been our pattern for a long time. These habits began in childhood and grew more embedded and automatic over the course of our lives. By our twenties this became the only way we knew how to think, and we were stuck in patterns of reacting to ourselves and to others that for some can be highly dysfunctional. On a day-to-day basis many of these latent patterns run as background conversation in our minds.

Take my friend with cancer for instance. Until his diagnosis, he had the typical worries about his kids, his business, the future of the country, and so on. These resided on the "back burner" like an old smoldering fire that would never fully die. Then one day he visited a doctor for an examination and was told that he had cancer. The immediate shock of this negative surprise was like pouring gasoline on an already smoldering fire. Old patterns of thinking and reacting were immediately triggered, and he became consumed in stress, intense fear, and worry. His thoughts were on the past—regrets, things he should have taken care of but didn't, and so on. Or at times they shifted ahead to the uncertain future. He would ask himself, "How much time do I have? What about my company? What about my kids and grandkids? Where will this all end and how much will I suffer from the treatments?"

With no effort at all on his part, this man could easily be swallowed up by an incessant, involuntary, and largely negative stream of thoughts that he cannot control. Thus he would not only suffer from a physical disease and its attending discomforts and illness, but on top of that, a heavy burden of stressful thoughts as well. His suffering would be multiplied into both intense physical and mental suffering.

Like this man, each of us could benefit from increased awareness, especially at stressful times. Mindfulness is actually nothing more than paying attention, on purpose. This sounds so easy. Who doesn't pay attention? How hard can that really be? When you pay attention on purpose, you immediately notice that your mind is either dwelling on the past or the future, not the precious present, where life actually takes place. Thus, the present eludes you as thoughts of the past or future intrude on the now so that you are not living fully in the present moment but caught somewhere in time.

We cannot live fully in the present if our minds are elsewhere. When we realize that all we really have is now, the pull of the past or fear of the future subsides and we begin to grow in present awareness. So many people are never really happy because their thoughts are somewhere else, either before or after the present moment. They can't enjoy today because of old thoughts spilling into the present or fears of the future pressing down on them. Mindfulness enables us to be where we are right now, fully aware and engaged with the precious present. This focus is how we interrupt the stream of stressful, compulsive thoughts that derive power from our lack of attention.

As your awareness increases, you will also notice that your mind is constantly judging your present experience. When my friend with cancer learned of his diagnosis, his mind immediately made a judgment about the experience, labeling it as a terrible setback, a tragedy, a punishment from God for previous mistakes, or as something else entirely from the countless other possibilities available. When we judge our present experience, it immediately shifts our attention away from the present into the past or future. The mind's tendency to judge is one of its most predictable reactions. When we judge ourselves, others, God, or any external situation, we immediately bring upon us various negative emotions. The intense emotional pressure that trials and stern setbacks bring flows from our judgments of these situations. To judge something as a terrible tragedy or the worst possible thing you could ever imagine happening to you is both negative and counterproductive. And the feelings that will follow such a judgment are easy to predict. They are self-defeating, stressful, and prevent us from paying attention to the present and acting with wisdom in the moment.

When we judge our present experiences, we think things should be different from how they really are. We may say something like, "This shouldn't be happening to me—I've been healthy my entire life." To resist reality in any way is stressful, yet we do it all the time. Whenever we think things should be different from how they are, we resist and resent the present reality. This will always generate within us negative and stressful feelings.

Think of a frustrated new mother who is annoyed and stressed out because her newborn wakes up three times a night, interrupting her sleep.

"Why doesn't she just go to sleep and stay asleep?" she complains to her mother. "This baby is making me crazy. I thought newborns slept a lot. What's her problem?"

"Well, honey," says her mother trying to reassure her, "this is often what new babies do, so you better get used to it. All my babies were like that for a while. Some are better sleepers than others."

"Well, I don't like it!" her daughter snaps. "I hate being woken up three or four times a night! She needs to learn to sleep clear through the night."

We can either accept reality or resist it, and when we resist it for whatever reason, we disturb ourselves. The baby isn't annoying this new mother or causing her frustration. Instead her feelings are caused by the thoughts that originate inside her own head as she judges her experience as "stupid, ridiculous, and unacceptable." Of course no amount of judging or feeling bad will improve matters. She will continue to be disturbed and stirred up by her current situation until she stops judging it as bad and wrong. This is what the mind does, far more than we realize. It turns everything into a problem, and when it does, you can be certain your thoughts resist reality as it is, right now at that moment.

A more mindful response would be, "It is what it is. I'm doing all I know how to help my baby sleep, and hopefully she'll grow out of it and start sleeping through the night soon." Refusing to judge her present situation frees this mom from the stress, frustration, and resentment that trying to oppose her reality naturally brings. One message that negative feelings of any kind affirms is that we are judging something or someone, wanting reality to be different from how it actually is. But all the resentment the young mother can muster won't change her baby's sleeping habits, although the tension between them might increase, interrupting everybody's sleep.

Eckhart Tolle declares, "Life is empty and meaningless. It is what it is. It is not bad or sad or terrible or horrible or horrific. It just is . . . and the mind judges it, labels it and by so doing creates pain because of a desire to think things should be different from how they actually are. Observe the mind, think about your thinking, listen to its patterns and you step out of its resistance pattern. This allows the present moment to simply be as it already is, without resistance. Always work with the present moment, not against it. Make it your friend, not your enemy."[2]

We have mentioned in other parts of this book the opposing ideas of holding on to a thought, idea, or story versus letting go. Sometimes we've clung to a story or belief for so long it's hard to let it go. It feels as much a part of us as our hearts or hands. Learning to let go of our attachment to long-held ideas, stereotypes, beliefs, and stories is part of the magic of mindfulness. We may hold on to old memories, stories, or difficult experiences that we simply feel we can't overcome. We may think, *I need to let this go*, but then the more we try, the more it persists. Then we compound the problem by judging ourselves for not being able to move past a painful memory or difficult experience. Letting go involves letting things be. Allow such thoughts to arise as they will and instead of judging them or trying to push them away, observe them as the watcher of your mind. Notice where they go, what other thoughts rise up, what feelings are generated, and your internal reactions to the thought. The mind so naturally judges that even our attempts to let an old memory go will be judged by the mind.

Thoughts may appear such as, "You can't let this go. It's impossible. You're naïve if you think you can simply get over this. Forget it. Just try to cope with it the best you can." Often any attempt to transcend the stressful mind or keep it from doing what it does will evoke a strong negative reaction from the voice in your head. It's as if a part of us resists our efforts to change and grow. This is yet another example of how fallen mortals naturally think, often in very devilish and self-defeating ways. Mindful to this automatic pattern, we can observe it and see its effects on us emotionally and spiritually. By shining the light of awareness on such thoughts, they lose power over us. We "put off" the natural mind doing what it does when we stand back from the strong current of incessant thought, rather than allowing ourselves to be swept along by it, clueless to what's happening. Thus, as we have said before, increasing our awareness of what our minds are doing is and absolutely critical to ridding ourselves from the burden of stressful thoughts and the disturbing, burdensome emotions they produce.

There is a vast difference between your authentic eternal self and the chaotic, often stressful stream of thoughts running constantly through your head. Tolle suggests that we learn to be the "watcher of the thinker."[3] Notice what's running through your mind. Pay attention to the pattern of the thoughts that arise so easily when you think about certain things. Notice how random and chaotic these thoughts can be, popping off on any topic from Brazil to peanut butter, with no apparent connection. You'll soon realize that this strange and often bizarre and endless stream of thought is not you. You can witness it and step back from it, like a bystander observing a nearby conversation. Simply notice what's running through your head. Be mindful of the chatter within.

Let's face it, most of us move through our days generally unaware of the thinkers inside our heads. Unaware of their running commentary, or just accustomed to it, we become oblivious to what they're saying. We are oblivious to the constant commentary on, opinions about, and judgments of the people and circumstances around us. This lack of awareness may not create a problem until we face a difficult life event, like a setback, a negative surprise, or an intense challenge. At such times the rush of our internal rivers of thought intensifies greatly, and the speed with which thoughts rush upon us is nearly impossible to avoid. Caught up by the current, we are swept along to think, react, and feel in very stressful ways. The key to everything we have been discussing is to become increasingly more mindful of what's happening inside our heads, especially at difficult times.

Mindfulness is a practice best developed in non-stressful times. Place your attention on any normal activity—much like the raisin exercise. Be more mindful when you are doing things like taking a shower, walking up stairs, shopping in the mall, exercising, shaving, talking on the phone, or something similar. Pay attention to what's happening around you and within you. Notice your thought patterns, reactions, judgments, and opinions if any arise. Pay attention to the details in what you are doing. Place your full awareness on the smallest details in a standard activity. You'll soon realize, as did the people who performed the raisin exercise, that much of life is run on autopilot.

An easy way to become more mindful is to sit down and simply pay attention to your breathing; notice how you inhale and exhale. Notice the air coming into your nose and feel it as it moves in and out of your nostrils. Notice the rise and fall of your chest and belly. Try to focus only on your breathing for two minutes. You'll notice a couple things. First that it's difficult and unnatural to be so mindful. Few of us take even two minutes a day to be mindful. Caught up in the rush of life, we are constantly doing, rarely being aware. You'll also notice that thoughts of various kinds begin to spin up inside your head. You might even have thoughts like, *This is silly. What am I doing sitting here doing nothing? I have too much to do to just sit here.* You'll realize through this small exercise that you, the real you, is much larger than the silly thoughts popping up inside your head. You can separate yourself from your thoughts. You can become the "watcher of the thinker." Notice your thoughts and reactions. Pay attention to any thoughts you have about your thoughts, which is the mind doubling back on itself for another round of thinking, judging, and commentary. This is not you. It's merely the natural mind doing what it does, with no conscious effort whatsoever on your part.

As you grow increasingly more mindful, you will be able to distinguish yourself from the thoughts running in your head. You'll see that your thoughts are a small subset of the vast essence of your divine character, the essential you. You are something more, behind or beneath the stream of thoughts running through your head. Soon you'll be able to distinguish two distinct entities—the thought and you, the casual bystander, observing it, noticing it, and aware of it. This is the beginning of freedom and the moment when you begin to awaken from the sleep of mindlessness. Learn to observe your thoughts, notice your feelings, and observe your reactions.

I had a conversation recently with Karen, a woman who is in my ward but never attends church. As we talked about her reasons and concerns for not coming, she spoke of a variety of fears. "I'm afraid you'll call on me if I come to your class. I'm afraid I'll look stupid. I'm afraid I'll run into Jenny, and she and I haven't spoken in years since our dog killed one of their rabbits. And when I do come, I sit and wonder if everyone is judging me for not coming to church more often."

This woman is swallowed up by her stressful thoughts of which she is completely unaware. She knows she has these feelings but can't separate herself from this stream of thought and the negative reactions it produces.

I suggested she work on becoming more mindful. "When you

come to church, I want you to notice several things. Be aware of your thoughts, opinions, judgments, and reactions to what happens, and to those around you. Pay more attention to your reactions to others than simply what others say or do. I want you to keep your attention fixed inside on your own thoughts—on the stream of thought that often disrupts your peace and keeps you from doing what you really want to do. Please notice what's happening inside your head and after church, tell me what you have found."

The very fact that we are not our thoughts and that we can observe them is a profound idea for many people. "You are not your thoughts, Karen," I told her. "This is just what your mind does. It thinks, throws up opinions, makes judgments, agrees, and disagrees—but that is not you. You can step back and observe all of that and be far more than just the stream of thought. You have the capacity to observe and notice what's happening inside you, to see your automatic reactions and their impact on you and others."

After church I followed up with Karen. "So tell me, what did you notice running around your head?"

"It was weird," she said with some excitement. "A lot of what I think is about fear. I'm afraid of what people think, afraid you'll ask me a hard question, afraid of what others will think when I can't answer your questions, afraid they'll ask me to talk or teach or visit someone I don't like. I have a lot of fearful thoughts inside my head."

"That's great, Karen," I said, equally excited. "Now remember, all that stuff isn't you. That's just your mind spinning away, based on old experiences, worries about the future, distorted beliefs about what might happen, and so on. And how do we know that this fearful stuff isn't really you? Because you can watch it, see it spinning along, and realize that this is not the way you want to be. And if we took the next step, we would discover that most of the things you think about so automatically aren't even true. It's all like a bad dream that you get caught up in when you fail to step back and notice what's happening inside your head. But the more aware you become, the more often you wake up from the nightmare of stressful thoughts and stories."

The more aware we are of our minds' reactive and habitual patterns, the less power they have to control us. When we are not swallowed up by the contents of our minds, we grow in awareness, which decreases the power of our thoughts over ourselves and our lives. Fear, anxiety, worry, anger, judgment, blame, agitation, or discouragement all occur in the mind. In the world, there are no problems. All problems are created in the mind by how it thinks about situations, explains what they mean, and projects how they will impact us today and in the future.

This is the key insight of this book: There are no problems, only thoughts, judgments, stories, and opinions. If a man loses a job, that means nothing until his mind spins out a series of thoughts that infuse meaning into it. Take any event, as difficult and stressful as you can imagine. Notice your reactions to this event. Notice your thoughts about it, the stories you begin to spin about what it means, and how it will impact you and others. This is all mind stuff, mental meanderings that we all do. Now become aware of these patterns running in your head. Pay attention to feelings, for they are the physical reflection of the mind in the body. Stressful, burdensome feelings can be a useful reminder to go within and observe your stressful mind at work. The very act of watching your mind diminishes its power over you. In that moment when you think, "This is a huge problem—a disaster," go inside your mind, be still, and watch the thinker. It's always running; it has no off button, so you will never look inside your head and find nothing there. Negative feelings signal that what is happening in your head is distorted and negative, essentially judgmental in nature.

If we honestly want to rise above the common stress and strain of life, we must learn to become more aware, more mindful than we usually are. Remember, there are no problems and there is no such thing as stress; there are only thoughts. There are no problems in the world, only inside your head as your habitual, incessant mind generates problems out of everything.

If this is true, we face an interesting prospect. If all present problems and concerns were suddenly taken away, what would happen? That depends on your level of mindfulness. If you have not learned to watch your inner thinker and be aware of the stressful thoughts that drive your negative reactions, you would soon create a new set of problems to replace the old. The mind and its stressful patterns would put you right back where you started.

The truth is simple. The more aware we are, the fewer problems we experience, since after all, problems occur in our heads, not in the world. Those who are mindful can stand apart from the natural, stressful reactions and respond with wisdom and choice, not act out of old automatic patterns. Mindfulness allows us to feel peace amid great trial and afflic-tion. We set ourselves apart from our circumstances and rise above them through our awareness of a broader purpose and through deeper realiza-tions of who we really are.

SOME SUGGESTIONS

Mindfulness must be developed since it is unnatural, amid our busy lives, to be aware, pause to notice, step back, and observe the thinkers inside our heads and their impact on our lives. Here are a few sugges-tions I've found useful for putting the ideas in this chapter into daily practice.

1. Begin a regular mindfulness practice as soon as possible. You can do this in the privacy of your own home, or you can take a class. It doesn't matter how or where you begin, but it is critical that you begin. The work of Dr. Jon Kabat-Zinn is as good as any I have ever used. Since we are so naturally unaware, it requires conscious, deliberate practice to go within and notice. Learning how to be mindful in any aspect of life is very powerful. That's where our peace can be found and the place where we can go when the experiences of life begin to overwhelm us.

    One specific practice you can begin tonight is a simple "recapture and review" exercise. Before retiring to bed, reflect on the day. Review the most significant events of the day and write them down in a journal. Try to focus on those experiences that held the most power—positive or negative. Write them all down. In the morning, when you first awaken, write down whatever you recall from your dreams. Not the meaningless stuff that we all have but anything in your dreams that was meaningful or strikes you as important. This simple exercise helps you capture what you might otherwise dash through without a second thought. It helps you learn to pay attention to the daily experiences of your life and note your reactions more mindfully.

2. All meditation practices I am aware of use breathing as a point of focus. Close your eyes and notice your breathing. Breathing in and out slowly, deliberately, and mindfully helps turn the

volume down on your internal commentator. Lie quietly on the floor with a small pillow and simply pay attention to your breathing. This will help you see how incessant the thinker within in you really is, especially when you're trying to weaken its pull on you. Thoughts will arise out of nowhere as they always do. You'll find it hard to not be distracted by this endless stream of random thoughts. But gently return to your breathing, always your breathing, as the place to center you and bring you back from any mental distractions. If you can carve out only ten minutes a day at first, this will still be a powerful beginning to a critical centering process, especially when you feel stirred up and stressed out.

3. Strive to be more aware wherever you go and whatever you do. When standing in line at the bank, be aware of your breathing and then notice your stressful thoughts about people at banks, lines, slow tellers, and so on. Step away from the stressful stream of thought and just notice it. Don't judge it or analyze it to death. Simply notice your thoughts, reactions, and feelings. Then remind yourself this is normal and that by doing what you just did, you invited peace into an otherwise stressful daily experience. The more you do this, the more natural it will become, and your negative feelings of stress will automatically subside.

4. Spend time in nature. Nature makes it easier to calm down and reflect. Grow intensely interested in everything around you and within you. The smells, the sights, the sounds. Notice all of it. Drink it in without any attempt to judge it, label it, or even think about it. Just be present and aware—nothing more. People often find a walk in nature very relaxing. This is because their mental strain diminishes when they take their thoughts off their mind, pay attention to beauty, and experience the awe and reverence that nature often instills. Once you learn to do this in the solitude of nature, begin to practice it in everyday life where it really counts, under the pressure of your daily experiences. Rise above the stressful internal chatter and wake up to the peace that surrounds you when you disconnect from your involuntary compulsive mind.

Notes

1. Jon Kabat-Zinn, *Full Catastrophe Living: Using the Wisdom of Your Body and Mind to Face Stress, Pain, and Illness* (New York: Random House), 29.

2. Eckhart Tolle, *Practicing the Power of Now: Essential Teachings, Meditations, and Exercises from The Power of Now* (Novato, California: New World Library Audio, 2003), book on CD. See also Eckhart Tolle, *The Power of Now* (Novato, California: New World Library, 1999).

3. Ibid.

ACKNOWLEDGMENTS

Anyone who writes a book depends on a strong supporting cast to pull it all together. I am indebted to Rachel Merkley and Kendra Arbon for their editing assistance as we drew near the end of this project. Had they not been available, I would still be stuck on page thirty-three, wondering how to spell tribulation! Also, my daughter Karianne Klomp eagerly offered her time and wisdom on the content of the book, and was invaluable in helping me finalize it under tight deadlines. I could have never met the deadlines without her able and loving assistance. I thank her for all she does to assist me in countless ways on so many fronts.

If an author is the leading man of a very personal book like this, then my wife Cindy is certainly my leading lady. For thirty-one years, she has walked alongside me through the various ups and downs of life. Even though she is keenly aware of my imperfections, she treats me as if I am the most perfect man in the world. This book could have never been written had I not passed through the challenging experiences I did, and had she not been there to support me through it all. She is now, and has always been a wife for all seasons, for which I am eternally grateful.

Cindy and I have three remarkable married children who married three equally remarkable individuals. Thus far we have four grandchildren, with one on the way, and several more on back order! Nothing brings me greater joy than watching my own children , now parents raising their little ones "unto the Lord." How blessed I feel to be a father and grandfather. For their love, support, and assistance I offer my sincere gratitude and affection.

Finally, I have had several of phenomenal teachers who have made a significant difference in my life. Dr. Robert Pope, Rebecca Overson, and Jeanette Maw are three stellar examples. Each of these special and caring individuals has blessed my life in countless and profound ways. I could have easily written about trials and setbacks without their help, but could not have written much about making sense of them. My learning came about through their profound insight and power to teach and explain what I most needed to hear. Their wisdom and light shined on me during some of my darkest experiences. Their commitment to my learning was strong and unwavering. I thank each for all they have done to bless my life and by extension bless the lives of all who read this volume.

ABOUT
THE
AUTHOR

Randy J. Gibbs is an author, trainer, life coach, and health and fitness consultant. He earned a master's degree in social work in 1980 and worked as a family therapist. After earning a second master's in organizational behavior, Randy moved into the business world, but his focus on helping people create positive change remained his central passion.

Randy worked for several large companies as a corporate trainer and coach before launching his own coaching and consulting practice in 1995. All of this unfolded while Randy was legally blind. At age ten, he was diagnosed with a rare retina disease that left him legally blind and partially sighted. His eyesight limitations turned into intense interest in how we all see the world, and Randy discovered that while physical blindness has its challenges, a distorted inner vision can be even more devastating. Helping people see themselves and their life situations clearly is the essence of Randy's work. People who have worked with him say that even though his eyesight is less than perfect, his insight is keen and powerful. Randy has taught a variety of leadership and personal effectiveness seminars around the world and is best known as a powerful and engaging teacher.

Randy has served in various teaching capacities in the Church and currently serves as a Gospel Doctrine teacher and as an institute instructor at Brigham Young University. He is married to the former Cindy Brough, and they are the parents of three children with four grandchildren and counting. They live in Orem, Utah. You may contact Randy through email (randy@rjgibbs.com) or visit his website: rjgibbs.com.